Cult of Power

Sex Discrimination in Corporate America
and
What Can Be Done About It

Martha Burk

A LISA DREW BOOK

SCRIBNER

New York   London   Toronto   Sydney

A LISA DREW BOOK / SCRIBNER
1230 Avenue of the Americas
New York, NY 10020

SCRIBNER and design are trademarks of Macmillian Library Reference USA, Inc.,
used under license by Simon & Schuster, the publisher of this work.

A LISA DREW BOOK is a trademark of Simon & Schuster, Inc.

For information regarding special discounts for bulk purchases,
please contact Simon & Schuster Special Sales at
1–800–456–6798 or business@simonandschuster.com.

Designed by Kyoko Watanabe
Set in Sabon

Manufactured in the United States of America

1   3   5   7   9   10   8   6   4   2

Library of Congress Cataloging-in-Publication Data
Burk, Martha [date]
Cult of power: sex discrimination in corporate America
and what can be done about it/
Martha Burk.
"A Lisa Drew book."
Includes bibliographical references and index.
1. Sex discrimination against women—United States.
2. Sex discrimination in employment—United States.
3. Augusta National Golf Club. I. Title.

HQ1426.B845 2005
305.42'0973—dc22
2004061604

ISBN 0-7432-6450-9

For the women:
To Dorothy, for her love, iron-willed determination,
intelligence, and insistence on excellence.
To Gertrude, for her unconditional love and kindness,
and to Jewel, for her undying loyalty.

CONTENTS

Cult of Power

A Simple Letter—
About Discrimination, Not Golf

It all started routinely enough—with a simple three-paragraph letter, addressing a little-noticed issue in the eternal battle for gender equity. But it exploded into a cause célèbre that laid bare the ways in which, and the reasons why, women are still systematically barred from the highest echelons of power—in government, social and religious organizations, and most importantly, in corporate America. We would see all too starkly how corporate elites enforce the code of behavior that maintains their control, the strength of the conspiracy of silence that surrounds sex discrimination at high levels, and the depth of corporate hypocrisy with all its fancy rhetoric about fairness and how women are valued as equals. Far from being about a few rich females gaining admittance to one club, the gates of Augusta National Golf Club became symbolic of all the ways women are still kept out of power where it counts, and how and why we must change the system to break in.

But back to the beginning.

In April 2002, I was traveling to Texas from my home in Washington, D.C., to visit my adult children, and I picked up a copy of *USA Today*. Unlike many women who unceremoniously toss the sports section, I usually thumb through it to get an idea of how much coverage is given to female athletes and women's teams. This day was an attention grabber. Columnist Christine Brennan had a piece titled "Augusta Equality Fight: Pass It On," with an accompanying story by Debbie Becker headlined "Augusta faces push for women." The subject was the exclusion of women at Augusta National Golf Club. Augusta National, host of the prestigious Masters Golf Tournament opening that day, was one of the most venerated golf clubs in the world. It was also highly secretive. No one outside the clan of three hundred or so who got in "by invitation only" knew who the members were—but everyone knew there had never been a female among them. Brennan credited a compelling story by Marcia Chambers in *Golf for Women* as the reason she chose to devote her column—for the third year in a row—to the sex discrimination at Augusta, even though she felt her earlier efforts had been like "beating my head against a brick wall about the issue."

Brennan made it clear that corporate sponsors of the Masters (Coca-Cola, IBM, and Citigroup) were part of the problem, since they were willing to underwrite an event at a club that practiced sex discrimination, even though it went without saying they wouldn't go near a club that kept out blacks, Asians, or Hispanics. She called it *acceptable discrimination* versus *unacceptable discrimination*. Little did I know how deeply true that statement would turn out to be. Brennan had interviewed Lloyd Ward, an African American and one of only a handful of publicly known names on the secret membership list at Augusta National. Ward, who was head of the United States Olympic Committee, told her that rather than resign in protest, he was going to work from the inside to change the policy. I believed him.

As chair of the National Council of Women's Organizations (NCWO), the nation's oldest and largest coalition of women's groups, I take any report of discrimination seriously, and this was no exception. I tore the stories out of the paper, thinking we should help Ward's efforts along by writing to the club. I reasoned that if they thought their practices were getting attention outside the cloisters of the golf establishment, it would hurry their decision to open to women. Sitting in front of the television watching the end of the Masters two days later, I casually mentioned to my daughter-in-law that the club didn't admit women, and we were going to try to put some pressure on them to change.

It was not a new area of controversy. Private clubs and secret societies have existed in the United States since before the country's founding; some of them, like the Freemasons, were brought over by the colonists. The issue of whether those that restrict membership to certain groups—by definition, keeping out other groups—are harmful to society and infringe on the rights of the have-nots had emerged in a large way for women in the late twentieth century. Women were entering the business world in sufficient numbers to question exclusionary club policies as detrimental to their ability to advance on the same footing as men. *The New York Times* put it this way back in 1980, when women were litigating to open the doors of private clubs in New York:

This disadvantage [in business] stems from the summary exclusion of women from membership in men's clubs, wholly on the basis of their sex. Evidence strongly suggests that these clubs can be essential to professional achievement. In fact, approximately one-third of all businessmen obtain their jobs through personal contacts, and these clubs strive to create an atmosphere that cultivates business deals and contacts.[1]

In theory, private clubs may be extensions of a person's home, and therefore thoroughly private places. But in practice . . . they are often extensions of the marketplace and world affairs. The current effort in many places to strike down barriers against . . . women and others is not just an effort by once excluded groups to find new company where they aren't wanted. It is an effort to throw open the meeting grounds of business and politics and to eliminate, once and for all, barriers that are unquestionably rooted in discrimination.[2]

The New York case is illustrative of the history of private club discrimination, and legal efforts to end or amend it. It goes to the heart of the question of women's (and, earlier, minority men's) struggle to be accepted as equals in the business world. Private "social" clubs where business was done were particularly disdainful of the few women who made it to the upper echelons of business, and their policies were personally and professionally humiliating.[3, 4]

Muriel Siebert, the first woman to own her own seat on the New York Stock Exchange and at the time Superintendent of Banks for the State of New York, testified in 1973 before the New York City Commission on Human Rights that as a trainee she had for years been passed over when her bosses sent male colleagues to seminars and meetings at private clubs because they knew she would be excluded, and of current experiences such as having to enter the all-male Union League Club through the kitchen in order to attend board meetings of the Sales Executive Club.

When attending functions at the Locust Club in Philadelphia, a female member of the Philadelphia City Council was forced to eat in the basement, since female guests were seated separately from men for dining.

Jacqueline Wexler, president of Hunter College in New York, was removed from the lobby of the University Club by a doorman and ordered to wait in the vestibule to the ladies' room.

A black woman foundation trustee, also escorted out of the lobby of the University Club, observed that the insult was the same as she had experienced in being evicted from restaurants in the South, despite the genteel surroundings and absence of armed sheriffs.

A female executive of one of the country's largest public relations firms was barred from walking down the main stairway at Pittsburgh's Duquense Club with her CEO and the Fortune 500 board chairman to whom she had just made a presentation.

Female oil executives at the Lafayette Petroleum Club were forced to lunch alone while their colleagues joined other men in the main dining room. They were also forced to sit in the hallways to listen to speakers at monthly professional society meetings.[5]

Perhaps because Augusta National seemed a throwback that would surely follow other clubs into the twenty-first century with a little gentle persuasion, confronting the club was not a front-burner issue with me. NCWO has a broad agenda, and we were concentrating on a number of areas such as affirmative action, Social Security, child care, reproductive rights, and equality for women worldwide. Augusta could wait. I threw the clips in a folder for my next steering committee meeting, a month away. A couple of weeks later I met a woman named Rae Evans at a formal dinner in Washington. She told me she was a new member of the Ladies Professional Golf Association (LPGA) board, and I mentioned to her that we were probably going to write to Augusta National about their exclusion of women. She asked me to keep her in the loop.

When NCWO's steering committee met, the Augusta letter was the last thing on the agenda, and it was barely discussed. None of the steering committee members were golfers, and few followed sports other than Title IX issues. I explained the situation, including Ward's statement that he was going to work for change, and my conclusion that we could help his efforts along. Everyone said, "Okay, write a letter." It was so minor and so routine there was no reason even to take a formal vote.

I called Rae Evans and asked for a meeting because we didn't want to interfere if the LPGA already had some kind of dialogue going with Augusta National on opening to women. As an activist, I couldn't imagine that they wouldn't be protesting the situation. At our meeting, she told me that the LPGA did not have anything contemplated, and that she would not like to see street protests. I replied that we could do it either way—in quiet negotiations or in the streets—but that we intended to begin with a private letter. Although I truly didn't believe it would be necessary (I was still assuming the club would do the right thing), I did tell Evans that we were fully prepared to go to the sponsors. I knew that she could pass this information along to the golf establishment, and again I thought it would only hurry Augusta National's decision. She suggested that we copy the letter to James Singerling at the Club Managers Association of America, in addition to Lloyd Ward.

It took another month for me to get the letter written and distributed to the steering committee before mailing. It went out on June 12, 2002, and I pretty much forgot about it.

William Johnson
Chairman, Augusta National Golf Club
2604 Washington Road
Augusta, GA 30904

Dear Mr. Johnson:

The National Council of Women's Organizations (NCWO) is the nation's oldest and largest coalition of women's groups. Our 160 member organizations represent women from all socioeconomic and demographic groups, and collectively represent over seven million women nationwide.

Our member groups are very concerned that the nation's premier golf event, the Masters, is hosted by a club that discriminates against women by excluding them from membership. While we understand that there is no written policy barring women, Augusta National's record speaks for itself. As you know, no woman has been invited to join since the club was formed in 1932.

We know that Augusta National and the sponsors of the Masters do not want to be viewed as entities that tolerate discrimination against any group, including women. We urge you to review your policies and practices in this regard, and open your membership to women now, so that this is not an issue when the tournament is staged next year. Our leadership would be pleased to discuss this matter with you personally or by telephone. I will contact you in the next few weeks.

Sincerely,

Martha Burk, Ph.D., Chair

CC: James Singerling, Club Managers Association of America
CC: Lloyd Ward, United States Olympic Committee

When a letter arrived by FedEx from Augusta National on July 9, I was so busy I almost didn't open it. It was a terse three-sentence reply:

Dear Dr. Burk:

As you are aware, Augusta National Golf Club is a distinctly private club and, as such, cannot talk about its membership and practices with those outside the organization. I have found your letter's several references to discrimination, allusions to the sponsors and your setting of deadlines to be both offensive and coercive. I hope you will understand why any further communication between us would not be productive.

Sincerely,

William W. Johnson
Chairman

I tossed it aside, figuring I would deal with it later, mentioning to my assistant in passing that we got a kiss-off letter from Augusta National.

Ten minutes later, my phone rang. It was Doug Ferguson at the Associated Press, asking about Hootie Johnson's response to my letter. I was surprised to be getting any press call on this, much less from the AP, because try as we might to get attention for "women's issues," the press doesn't ring very often. Social Security and child care just aren't sexy enough topics. Anyway, I told Ferguson that I really hadn't had time to think about it, and that it was only three sentences telling me Johnson didn't want to communicate with me. Ferguson said he didn't mean *that* response, but the three-page press release the club had sent out. I told him I was unaware of a press release, so he read it to me for my reaction. (He also faxed it at my request after the interview, a tremendous help for what was to come.)

We have been contacted by Martha Burk, Chair of the National Council of Women's Organizations (NCWO), and strongly urged to radically change our membership. Dr. Burk said this change should take place before the Masters Tournament next spring in order to avoid it becoming "an issue." She suggested that NCWO's leadership "discuss this matter" with us.

We want the American public to be aware of this action right from the beginning. We have advised Dr. Burk that we do not intend to participate in such backroom discussions.

We take our membership very seriously. It is the very fabric of our club. Our members are people who enjoy each other's company and the game of golf. Our membership alone decides our membership—not any outside group with its own agenda.

We are not unmindful of the good work undertaken by Dr. Burk's organization in global human rights, Social Security reform, reproductive health, education, spousal abuse and workplace equity, among others. We are therefore puzzled as to why they have targeted our private golf club.

Dr. Burk's letter incorporates a deadline tied to the Masters and refers to sponsors of the tournament's telecast. These references make it abundantly clear that Augusta National Golf Club is being threatened with a public campaign designed to use economic pressure to achieve a goal of NCWO.

Augusta National and the Masters—while happily entwined—are quite different. One is a private club. The other is a world-class sports event of great public interest. It is insidious to attempt to use one to alter the essence of the other. The essence of a private club is privacy.

Nevertheless, the threatening tone of Dr. Burk's letter signals the probability of a full-scale effort to force Augusta National to yield to NCWO's will.

We expect such a campaign would attempt to depict the members of our club as insensitive bigots and coerce the sponsors of the Masters to disassociate themselves under threat—real or implied—of boycotts and other economic pressures.

We might see "celebrity" interviews and talk show guests discussing the "morality" of private clubs. We could also anticipate op-ed articles and editorials.

There could be attempts at direct contact with board members of sponsoring corporations and inflammatory mailings to stockholders and investment institutions. We might see everything from picketing and boycotts to T-shirts and bumper stickers. On the internet, there could be active chat rooms and email messaging. These are all elements of such campaigns.

We certainly hope none of that happens. However, the message delivered to us was clearly coercive.

We will not be bullied, threatened or intimidated.

Obviously, Dr. Burk and her colleagues view themselves as agents of change and feel any organization that has stood the test of time and has strong roots in tradition—and does not fit their profile—needs to be changed.

We do not intend to become a trophy in their display case.

There may well come a day when women will be invited to join our membership but that timetable will be ours and not at the point of a bayonet.

We do not intend to be further distracted by this matter. We will not make additional comments or respond to the taunts and gripes artificially generated by the corporate campaign.

We shall continue our traditions and prepare Augusta National Golf Club to host the Masters as we have since 1934.

> With all due respect, we hope Dr. Burk and her colleagues recognize the sanctity of our privacy and continue their good work in a more appropriate arena.

I was astounded by the tone and language in the press release, but I went ahead and did the AP interview, it's fair to say with zero preparation. Being only a casual golf fan and knowing some tournaments moved around year to year, I made one mistake: I said if Augusta National didn't open to women, perhaps the tournament should be moved. I didn't know, of course, that the club owns the Masters and it never moves, while the other PGA Tour events move every year. Ferguson printed the gaffe, and it was used against me repeatedly by those who disagreed with our position. Though the language differed, the essence was "What is she doing sticking her nose into golf? The dumb bitch doesn't even know Augusta National *owns* the Masters." Just in case anyone doubts that a double standard is alive and well, Jesse Jackson made the same mistake on television a month or so later, and not a single member of the press made an issue of it, or dared call him dumb or uninformed.

My phone continued to ring all afternoon. *The New York Times, The Atlanta Journal-Constitution, USA Today,* the *Los Angeles Times,* and many others called. I was on the radio and CNN by evening, but I still thought it was a one-day story. Boy, was I wrong. The media firestorm would continue for most of the next year. For better or worse, I would become a central figure in the controversy about power, money, gender, and exclusion that played out on hundreds of talk radio shows, dozens of television debates on all the major networks, and in the pages of *The New York Times, The Wall Street*

Journal, and *People* magazine, not to mention in kitchen table discussions and family arguments around the country.

Those that didn't get it thought we were making a big deal out of nothing—what difference does it make if a few rich guys get together and chase a little ball around? As feminists, it went without saying that we knew this was never about golf. It was about power, about keeping women out of places where important business is done, and most of all, about how sex discrimination is viewed in business circles and by extension in society at large. The press knew it, the club knew it, and judging from our e-mails, most of the public knew it too.

Tirades from both sides of the gender divide poured into our office—close to five hundred e-mails a day. Not all the men were against us, nor all the women for us. But all had strong opinions. On the one hand, it wasn't about golf, it was about why women ought not to serve in combat. It was about the Equal Rights Amendment that would emasculate men, and everyone being forced to use unisex toilets. It was about men wanting to pee behind the trees without women seeing them. It was about women being physically weaker, that's why they shouldn't be firefighters. It was about my wife (whom I'm speaking for), who doesn't make as much money as I do, so yes, she has to do the dishes after her workday; that's fair. It was about you feminists are on the wrong track because I'm a female college student and all this gender stuff was settled ages ago. It was about you cunts destroying the world for whites and red-blooded men who hate fags.

On the other side, it was about all the crap I have to put up with at work from that sorry guy who I trained and now makes more than I do. It was about why my husband picks up his socks when the maid comes but not when I'm doing the housework. It was about my wife getting docked for having to leave early to pick up our kid, but the guy next to her could leave to get his car fixed without penalty. It was that this will forevermore be about men and boys not wanting to give up any modicum of power, and our willingness, as women—like the frog in the pan of warm water on the stove—to remain comfy and confident in our pan of warm water, waiting . . . well, we all know what happened to the frog.

The Deep Divide

Gender Superiority in the Culture

Aided by the 24-hour news cycle and a huge sports press infrastructure, the Augusta National controversy hit an artery in American culture, and hopped the oceans to Japan, Australia, Great Britain, France, South Africa, and even Botswana. Brennan put it best in her next column: "Whether it's kickball in the school yard, charades at a dinner party or an exhibition tennis match in the early 1970s, there is no more fascinating matchup than the boys against the girls." For the next year, I would do nothing but argue the "girls' side," as the controversy became less about golf and more about sex roles, where women ought to be allowed to go, and women's place in a society that still doesn't take sex discrimination all that seriously.

To see how we got to this stage in the argument, we could probably go back to the beginning of time, but I'll just start with God and Moses. In telling Moses how to value women in comparison to men, God gave these guidelines:[6]

Age	Male Value in Shekels of Silver	Female Value
1 mo.–5 years	5	3
5–20	20	10
20–60	50	30
60 and above	15	10

It is unclear why older women became more valuable—their worth relative to men jumped from 3:5 to 2:3 on turning sixty. There are other places in the Bible where women are told not to usurp authority over a man (I Timothy 2), to submit to men's authority (I Corinthians), and to keep their mouths shut in church (I Corinthians). The Bible is also full of the notion of women as property, and it even lays out the best way to take females as slaves. I don't mean to be picking on Judeo-Christian history to the exclusion of other anti-woman theology, some much older. It's just that this is the tradition that has dominated religion in the United States since the Pilgrims landed.

> . . . It is Satan at work. Just as he looked around the Garden of Eden and saw it was too quiet and peaceful, he decided to use Eve to create chaos and go against God, which resulted in paradise lost. So it is with Augusta National. Satan is . . . using Eve to disrupt a nice, orderly and smoothly run place, and create chaos where there was peace.
>
> Letter from Augustus Nelms to
> *The Augusta Chronicle*, 4/4/2002

The belief in the superiority of males over females that is explicit in early religion and implicit in culture to this day may be partly rooted in the physical dominance needed to survive in times long past. Power came from control over one's environment, including the people in it. From power flows a sense of entitlement, ultimately leading to a belief in the superiority of the holders of power—historically men. It's probably fair to say that institutionalized dominance of the male gender in societies around the world has produced a general belief, on the part of men and women alike, that the male gender is superior. Though it is changing, female culture still has roots in relative powerlessness, lack of entitlement, and a sense that their gender is less valued by society.

The modern reality that mastodons no longer need to be slain and females don't need protection from plunderers and rapists of opposing tribes (except for the occasional opposing football team) hasn't changed the underlying culture as much as we would like. Sure, there are now sensitive men and strong, dominant women. But cut through the layers of the onion, and at the core you'll still find that "men are meant to be leaders, women are natural-born followers" is the working cultural hypothesis of gender relations. Manifestations can range from what we generally view as chivalry to outright misogyny, depending on how particular individuals interpret the cultural norms.

On the notion of gender superiority, most enlightened men would say that they don't believe males are superior, and at a rational level, they would be telling the truth. But at the gut level—what psychologists call *cultural conditioning*—men have been indoctrinated with the opposite view. Some of NCWO's heaviest mail came after I said, in an interview with *The New Yorker*, that denigrating women is a large part of male culture:

> . . . when men get together, denigrating women is often a part of the social interaction. When women get together, denigrating men is rarely done. It's just not even on the

radar screen. Even among the so-called strident feminists of the women's movement. We don't have anything to hide in that way, and men seem to.

Men DENIED THIS . . . The quote was actually part of a long conversation I had had with the reporter about locker room talk, the basis of feelings of gender superiority, and even the roots of homophobia. My point was merely that disdain for women and girls is impossible to get away from in this society, and some of it sinks in, regardless of an individual's vigilance or egalitarian upbringing. It sinks in on women as well as men. Consider the word *sissy* (derived from sister), used to taunt little boys who cry. Or the word *wuss*, used by men to denigrate each other, most of the time jokingly. Now, deconstruct the word. It's a cross between *woman* and *pussy*, used in situations where *woman* is either not derogatory enough or politically incorrect, and *pussy* is too strong for polite company. But the meaning is the same: You are womanlike, lesser, a *girlie man*. Even men who would never use these words have heard them all their lives; most have heard guys put each other down with much rougher gendered insults.

Individual men reading this analysis may be

> Humiliation of men by equating them with women was starkly illustrated in the 2004 prison scandals in Iraq, when Iraqi prisoners were forced by Americans to wear women's underwear. It was accepted by both sides that this was an effective form of degradation, and initial press reports focused on this more than physical abuse. *The New York Times* (May 8, 2004, A.11) also reported that American male inmates in Arizona were "made to wear women's pink underwear as a form of humiliation."

thinking, "Hogwash. I don't minimize women or feel superior to them. I was insecure in high school, never dated, and felt wholly inadequate in front of the girls. And I wasn't a good enough athlete to have the respect of the boys. I felt no control whatsoever, in fact the opposite." These guys would be right, so far as any given *individual's* experience might be concerned. But that doesn't mean the *cultural values and norms* don't reflect the larger truths. Just because an individual male isn't particularly powerful doesn't mean he wasn't indoctrinated by the culture to value power and to believe that males are the superior gender. Think about it. All of this society's major institutions are led by men—the government, military, churches, universities, corporations, labor unions, professional sports. Kids can't help but notice. Look at any collection of portraits of "venerable leaders," I don't care where—from civic organizations to the U.S. Congress—and what you will see is a sea of men, mostly white at that. It sinks in.

In July 2004, Governor Arnold Schwarzenegger of California disparaged opposing lawmakers with this statement: "If they don't have the guts to come up here in front of you . . . if they don't have the guts, I call them girlie men." When Schwarzenegger was called on to apologize, his spokesman said, "It's a forceful way of making the point to regular Californians that legislators are wimps . . . if they complain too much about this, I guess they're making the governor's point."

And whether individuals consciously know it or not, there is a sense of entitlement that comes from being a member of the dominant group, regardless of personal outcomes. It's a very, very rare male who would make an even exchange with women in society. Many men think they would want stereotypical women's roles: sitting at home eating bonbons while the male slaves away at the mine or in the office. But they would want this role *while remaining male.* Men may say women have a better deal, but give them the hypothetical opportunity to *become a female,* and see how they respond. The culture actually instills in most men the fear of being thought womanlike: It's the basis of homophobia, the basis of considering women lesser, which plays out in business situations, in the home, the churches, and countless other places every day. (It is no accident that some men "jokingly" drop tampons on the green when their buddies have made particularly bad golf shots.)

The Separate Gender Cultures

Sometimes when I'm driving and lose patience with another motorist, honk, curse, or push my way through a traffic jam, my husband will tell me I'm driving by the "men's rules," meaning more aggressively and with a higher need to "win" the traffic confrontation.

Our melting pot society is composed of subcultures, based on any number of criteria. There are subcultures built around hobbies, work groups, sports, entertainment, religion, and many other categories. But two of the overarching subcultures that are most salient are race and gender. The interesting thing about the gender subculture is that it spans not only its own male/female divide, but the racial divide(s) as well. While neither women nor men are monolithic, there is a "men's culture" that is common to the vast majority of men, and a "women's culture" that is common to the vast majority of women, whether they be black, white, or some other race or ethnicity.

The separate gender cultures start very early in life. From pink for girls to blue for boys, to Barbie computers that have less memory and less program capacity than Hot Wheels computers, through the marketing of football worship versus footwear worship to high schoolers, gender stereotypes are drilled into kids' brains. We're not talking here about biology; no one denies the physical differences (males are generally stronger, but most people don't know females have more muscle endurance and cope with pain better). In a world where neither strength nor stamina are very important in everyday living, the separate cultures are shaped far more by ingrained attitudes, family dynamics, societal systems and traditions, media, and peer pressure than they are by differing physical capabilities.

So what we end up with are men who like to hunt and fish, women who like to shop, and not a few crossover members for the other's gender-identified activities. Most people (including me) don't have a problem with this arrangement, so long as others are not hurt, demeaned, or devalued in the process. Men like to hang out with the boys at times, and women like to have dinner with the girls on occasion, but there is a difference between these very private associations (more about that later) and public acts that send a message about forced gender segregation as a way to reinforce gender superiority. One of the articles that men grabbed like a lifeline as validation that women should be kept out of Augusta National failed to make this distinction.

In the March 2003 issue of *Golf Digest*, David Owen, official biographer of Augusta National, in "The Case for All-Male Golf Clubs," began his article this way:

I infuriated a woman I know by showing her the following excerpts from a statement by Hootie Johnson, the chairman of Augusta National Golf Club: While men's golf clubs are diverse, their members have a common desire to create sustained bonds with other men . . . Men's golf clubs, through their enduring presence, offer a sense of rootedness, a common body of experience and knowledge, a sense of continuity . . . We are forever being told to give more energy, more time, to our marriage, our career, our children, our community. Men's golf clubs tell us to spend more time with our male friends.

Owen went on to tell how after his acquaintance called this "a stinking bunch of sexist junk," he then confessed to her that Johnson hadn't actually said those things, and that he had lifted them (with some modifications he didn't explain) from a popular book called *Girls' Night Out: Celebrating Women's Groups Across America.* He had tricked this woman by substituting "men" for "women," "male" for "female," and "golf clubs" for "groups" in a passage taken from the introduction to the book. He then deftly equated women's bridge and mah-jongg groups to Augusta National Golf Club. Though it was clear that the book's authors were referring to *small intimate gatherings of friends* when they used the word *group,* Owen deliberately ignored this and held the book out as "proof" that women felt the same way he did about large commercial male-only private clubs like Augusta National, and that in fact gender-segregated clubs were not only no big deal, but actually preferred by women and men alike. Owen's case was tantamount to saying that because ethnic minorities might seek one another's company at birthday celebrations and dinner parties, it's okay to officially bar them from restaurants and nightclubs—in fact they would probably actually prefer it that way.

Nevertheless, men held Owen's article out like a talisman. One man in particular, Jerry Tarde, editor-in-chief of *Golf Digest,* hammered me repeatedly with it in a meeting I had been invited to with his editors and writers. The next issue of the magazine had a well-conceived article by Thomas Friedman making the case that Augusta National should open to women because it had become a national institution, and it should take moral leadership and do what was right, not hide behind what was nominally legal. But Tarde didn't want to talk about that. I couldn't tell him that I had been approached by one of his employees three months before about his own membership in Pine Valley, another all-male country club. The woman had been shaking and near tears when she told me that Tarde routinely entertains male staff and high-ranking officials from the ruling bodies of golf at Pine Valley, and she could not attend, though her rank at the magazine would dictate that she be included. When I told her that this type of exclusion could well be actionable—particularly if the prospects of women employees' advancement at the company would be seriously impaired by this exclusion—and she could sue, she said she needed the job and didn't want to be run out of sports journalism forever.

Owen's flawed premise and Tarde's defense of it are perfect examples of how cultural differences have been used to justify discrimination through the ages. Tarde's blatant discrimination against female employees, while using a male-only "private" club for business, is one more example of why it's not about friends getting together—and why it's sure as hell not about golf.

It's Perfectly Legal—Or Is It?

For a variety of reasons, including lack of resources, NCWO did not consider pursuing Augusta National legally. But it was mainly because we naively assumed that pressure on the sponsors would result in the club opening to women if our letter, combined with urging from members like Lloyd Ward, failed to work. A number of attorneys offered to help with a legal case. Brenda Feigen, a feminist lawyer from California who had worked with Ruth Bader Ginsburg in litigating sex discrimination cases for the ACLU in the 1970s, was especially keen to nail the club legally. She quietly put a tremendous amount of resources into investigating the possibilities, but ultimately concluded that while it was far from clear that Augusta National was within its legal rights as it claimed so loudly, NCWO could not survive the first courtroom hurdle, which would be a "motion to dismiss." This was because we would have had to appear before Judge Dudley Bowen, a known ally of Augusta National and its members. (Indeed, when NCWO challenged Augusta's city ordinance limiting our right to protest, Judge Bowen ruled against us on Thursday and entertained Augusta members at his aptly named Bull Haven Ranch on the following Saturday morning.)

We always made the moral argument: Sex discrimination is wrong, it shouldn't be practiced in high-level places where business is done, and places that brag about discriminating shouldn't be showcased on television and underwritten by corporate America. Though NCWO never challenged the club on legal grounds, the question of legality loomed large in the national discussion from the beginning. Augusta National had laid the groundwork with nine "talking points" to the press, headed by this one, which inadvertently referred to the Masters instead of the club:

> *This is not a legal issue. The Masters has a constitutional right to its private membership.*

The club's strategy was twofold: assert that it was operating within the law in barring women, and avoid the moral question by casting the conflict as one about the right to private association. Johnson equated the absence of lawbreaking with moral rightness and vindication—if it's legal it must be acceptable. (I call this kind of thinking the "Meese standard," after Edwin Meese III, attorney general under Ronald Reagan. When the independent counsel concluded a fourteen-month investigation just short of indicting Meese, he declared himself "completely exonerated.")

The second strategy—make it about private association—proved most effective. Talk radio (appropriately dubbed "the moronathon" by my able assistant Rebecca Menso) was awash in invective about the right to have a backyard barbecue without interference, and the right to have friends of your own choosing. Tiger Woods seemingly validated this point of view (and drew screaming headlines of criticism) when, asked if the club should admit women, he declared, "Everybody has a right to do what they want. Is it unfair? Yes." The fact that equating Augusta members—an international roster of some three hundred leaders in business, government, philanthropy, and the media who control millions of jobs, billions in government contracts, and budgets larger than many countries—with friends at a backyard barbecue was a deeply flawed comparison did not, of course, make a difference in the way many connected it to their personal "rights" and private behavior.

Ironically, the club had successfully used a tactic from the 1970s women's movement. Back then we called it *the personal is political.* The idea was to get women to make the connection between their personal lives and what was happening at a more systemic level. Access to credit is a good example. In those days, women were routinely denied credit in their own names. They had to get a male cosigner on promissory notes, even if said male was neither a spouse nor any more creditworthy than the female applicant. Prior to the 1970s, many women assumed that they were just unlucky in drawing an especially picky bank officer, or that they really were falling short on lending-institution criteria. The women's movement, with its "consciousness raising," made women see that if they couldn't get credit in their own name, it wasn't an isolated personal failing that applied only to an individual's particular circumstance. It was because *gender bias was built into the system.* There was an assumption that only men were capable of paying back loans (female borrowers needed a male "guardian"), and there was no prohibition on banks from engaging in biased lending practices. The *personal is political* part came when sufficient numbers of women realized that the *personal* inability to get credit was really a *political* problem that could be addressed through collective action. Women demanded change—resulting in the Equal Credit Opportunity Act of 1974.

Hootie Johnson had used the personal is political idea too—only he turned it upside down. In Augusta National's worldview, the *political* question (discrimination in society) was recast in *personal* terms (the right to association), which didn't exactly fit the situation, but most people could relate to it.

So what about the right to choose your friends and invite them to that barbecue? Indeed, the right to choose one's friends and associates is a strongly held American value, central to the notion of private association, individual freedom, and self-determination. And besides, the First Amendment guarantees the right to private association, doesn't it? Well, not exactly. Just as there is no explicitly stated right to abortion in the Constitution (it's implied in the right to privacy under the Fourteenth Amendment), there is actually no explicit guarantee of private association. The First Amendment guarantees "the right of the people peaceably to assemble." Courts have ruled in some circumstances that the right to private association is implied in this right to assembly. But courts have also established that we can claim this right to private association only *up to a point*—usually where it comes into conflict with a compelling state interest, such as overcoming discrimination in society. In general, whether a club is deemed private enough to enjoy protection under what courts call the right to "intimate" association depends on the answers to two questions: (1) Is the club truly private? (If yes, it's protected.) And (2) Is the club actually not so private, but merely using the "private" designation as a cover for discrimination? (If yes, it's not protected.)

Most people assume that women have some kind of constitutional protection against discrimination, because the Fourteenth Amendment guarantees equal protection of the law to all citizens.[8] But the Equal Protection Clause, adopted to give black men—but not women—the right to vote, prohibits only "state action" in discrimination. That means governments themselves cannot discriminate, nor can they facilitate discrimination by private organizations (e.g., give special tax breaks to organizations that discriminate). However, equal protection does not apply to discrimination by private individuals, groups, or organizations such as clubs or corporations.

Congress attempted to redress non-government discrimination with the Civil Rights Act of 1964 (more about that later), but women were left out of the federal public accommodations portion of the law, which prohibits discrimination in restaurants, hotels, and the like, but also specifically exempts private clubs. Title II of the Civil Rights Act of 1964 states the following: "All persons shall be entitled to the full and equal enjoyment of all goods, services, facilities, privileges, advantages and accommodations of any place of public accommodation, as defined in this section, without discrimination or segregation on the ground of race, color, religion, or national origin." Courts have apparently not considered women "persons" under this Title, even though it has been used to open some private clubs to black men, when such clubs can be shown to be operating as public accommodations. Unless they *can* be shown to be operating as public accommodations, private clubs are specifically exempt from

Title II anyway, creating a double barrier for women seeking relief under this statute.

Because of these relatively weak federal protections, many states (not including Georgia) have passed their own public accommodations laws to fortify the right to be free from discrimination for historically disadvantaged groups. Most include sex as a protected category and define public accommodation broadly enough that many so-called "private" clubs fall under their purview. Women have depended on these state (and sometimes local) laws to gain access to the business opportunities afforded by private clubs. Although many lawsuits have been filed (and some are ongoing), the current legal landscape is defined by a handful of cases.

The three most prominent cases all reached the Supreme Court with challenges to state or local public accommodations laws against discrimination. The claims were that these laws were unconstitutional restrictions of the right to private association. Rulings, while somewhat different, all strengthened women's access to private clubs and the business opportunities they provide. In *Roberts v. United States Jaycees* (which challenged the Minnesota Human Rights Act in 1984), the U.S. Jaycees tried to use free speech and private association arguments to keep women from holding memberships on equal footing with men. The Court ruled the Jaycees were not substantially burdened by giving women equal rights, and that Minnesota's interest in combating sex discrimination outweighed whatever associational rights the Jaycees could claim.[9] The Jaycees' arguments failed because their club met none of the criteria for what the Court defined as "intimate association": The organization was large, even within its local branches, it had a commercial purpose, and granting women the right to participate under some circumstances undermined any argument that the nature of the group required an all-male atmosphere. Finally, it was unselective in judging and admitting prospective members. (It is obvious that Augusta National Inc., a for-profit corporation that only "does business as" a golf club while producing a multimillion-dollar public sporting event, and even boasts about letting women participate but bars them as members, would fail all but the last test, if taken to court under a similar law to Minnesota's.)

The Roberts case was soon followed by *Board of Directors of Rotary International v. Rotary Club of Duarte*. The case was actually sparked by the admission of women by the Duarte chapter, which caused the parent group to revoke its charter. Duarte sued under the Unruh Civil Rights Act in California. And Duarte won—meaning the Court ruled that the relationships within Rotary were not of the intimate, familial type protected by the Constitution, and that admitting women would not substantially alter or disrupt its purpose.[10] So *Rotary* expressly limited "intimate association" protection to close family relationships,[11] a test Augusta National obviously could not pass.

New York City broke new ground in 1984 when it amended its Human Rights Law, which prohibited discrimination in places of public accommodation, to cover private clubs under certain conditions. This was the first case where

> Of all the issues I've been involved in, this is one I thought we'd put to rest.
>
> Lynn Hecht Schafran, Counsel of Record for Amici Curiae in *New York State Club Association v. City of New York* (U.S. Supreme Court, 1988), commenting on the insistence by Augusta National that exclusion of women is right and proper

the law directly limited the right of private clubs to discriminate, simultaneously eliminating the need to *prove* that certain clubs were in fact public accommodations. New York simply *defined private clubs as public accommodations* if they had more than four hundred members, provided regular meal service, and habitually took money from nonmembers (directly or indirectly) for dues, space, meals, or use of the facilities or services. The New York State Club Association sued, charging the law as facially invalid and overbroad. They lost. The Court said that the three tests laid out in the law were sufficient to define a nonprivate organization. So *New York State Club Association v. City of New York* (1987) appears to have created a workable definition for commercial activity, and to have set an upper limit for the number of members a club can have and still claim a right of private association. A lower limit has not been established; Kansas law sets a one-hundred-member limit that has not been challenged in court. While Augusta National would clearly fail the meal service and money criteria for claiming privacy, its size (approximately three hundred members) has not been tested.

Clubs have been prevented from discriminating through other methods dictated by various government bodies. In the District of Columbia and a number of states and local jurisdictions, no establishment practicing discrimination can hold a liquor license. Given the choice between the booze and keeping out the broads, many venerable bastions of sexism like the Cosmos Club in Washington changed their policies. When in the 1980s states began to deny tax breaks to clubs with discriminatory policies (since this effectively forced taxpayers to underwrite exclusion), many changed. Others, like Burning Tree in

Maryland, decided to keep the male-only policy and forego the tax breaks they had enjoyed. To date, that decision has cost Burning Tree several million dollars. Augusta National serves liquor, but there are apparently no licensing rules that apply. The club gets preferential treatment underwritten by taxpayers from the city, county, and state police departments, which provide services the club doesn't pay for every year during the Masters tournament. Rumor has it that the city also provides *free water* year round to maintain those beautiful azaleas and gorgeous greens. But Augusta, Georgia, is a company town, so nobody complains.

There is one form of private association that has been upheld by the courts—even for very large groups that can't possibly be a gathering of friends. The Court has called this *expressive association*. That is, when a club has a general mission to advocate a point of view (e.g., NAACP or KKK), it may legally bar individuals or groups that would have a significant effect on the group's ability to advocate those viewpoints.[12] So the NAACP does not have to admit the Grand Wizard of the KKK. Ironically, Augusta National most often compared itself to the Boy Scouts, who won their expressive association case against admitting homosexuals because they said they did not want to advocate homosexuality. But for a club like Augusta National to be able to discriminate against women and have expressive association protection, it would have to claim that its expressive purpose was something like male bonding or male superiority.[13] Augusta National has been unwilling to make that claim, at least explicitly. To the contrary, members state that they have nothing against women (no doubt some of their *best friends* are women) and might want to admit them someday.

But enough about Augusta's disingenuous comparison of itself to the Boy Scouts and sewing circles. What really matters to women in the United States today is how we got to the place where a powerful group of men could even *make* the argument that sex discrimination is okay, and have America's largest corporations backing them up.

Corporate America Closes Ranks

By the third press call from a reporter on that first day—immediately after I talked to the AP's Doug Ferguson and Cliff Brown of *The New York Times*—I understood something that no doubt kept this story alive in the beginning: Augusta National was not popular with members of the media. In response to my wondering out loud how Hootie Johnson ever got the inflammatory press release past his board, David Markiewicz of *The Atlanta Journal-Constitution* put it bluntly: "You don't understand. Hootie pretty much *is* the board. And a more arrogant son of a bitch you will never meet." In the next weeks it became clear that many reporters and opinion writers (and remember, the sports press corps is 90 percent male) were interested in seeing the club get its comeuppance. While a few were genuinely offended by the sex discrimination practiced by the club, the majority reacted to the "trouble in River City" with glee because Augusta National had treated individual reporters and news organizations alike with extreme arrogance over the years. Either way, it gave NCWO some allies we hadn't expected.

Not that we were all that concerned that we would need allies. Johnson's "Point of a Bayonet" press release had actually laid out a pretty standard campaign, beginning with pressure on the sponsors of the Masters. We had always known going to the sponsors was a possibility, and now was the time to move toward that step, which we thought would be the last one. We reasoned that no sponsor would stick with Augusta National once we made it clear that national women's groups were watching. After all, they marketed to women every day and had thousands of female employees; they couldn't very well sanction sex discrimination by underwriting an event at a place that proudly kept women out. They would pressure the club to open to women as a condition of continued sponsorship. The club would capitulate to retain the sponsorship money, and to avoid an embarrassing public announcement of sponsor withdrawal.

At this point the situation was an exact parallel to one that had occurred a dozen years earlier, when the subject was race. The Shoal Creek Country Club in Alabama was scheduled to host the 1990 PGA Championship, and the club president made a public statement that "we don't discriminate in any other area, except for blacks." Pressure on Shoal Creek to open to African Americans mounted quickly and forcefully. Some sponsors, including IBM, pulled out immediately, and the ABC network hinted that it would not broadcast the event. Pickets were threatened by the Southern Christian Leadership Conference. Within weeks the club capitulated and announced its first black member. The ruling bodies of golf—the PGA, the United States Golf Association, and the PGA and LPGA tours—adopted new policies: No tournaments would be held at venues that discriminated on the basis of race or gender. The championship went forward as planned, and institutional condemnation of discrimination had been strongly affirmed. But we would learn during our struggle that despite public pronounce-ments and policies on paper, it had been a racial barrier for men—but not the gender barrier—that had come down.

The PGA Tour, with its written policy of not holding tour-naments at discriminatory clubs, should have been a natural ally. They were—of Augusta National Golf Club. The Tour, more than any other group, including the players, members, and sponsors, had the power to force a change in Augusta's policy. By withdrawing the recognition it accorded the Mas-ters Tournament—meaning the tournament would no longer be counted in official player standings or official season win-nings as the other PGA Tour events were—the Tour could have ended the controversy almost before it began. But their response to our letter asking them to adhere to their own guidelines on discriminatory tournament sites was more evi-dence that Augusta National's influence was formidable.

> One of the peculiar things about the reaction to Johnson's stand is that he is getting solid support within the golfing community while the reaction of society at large is that the Augusta National members are living up to their worst stereotype: a bunch of rich, spoiled men who don't think women are worthy of their company.
>
> Ron Sirak, "The consensus is . . . ?" GolfWorld.com, 9/19/2002

Tour Commissioner Tim Finchem took a legalistic approach, stat-ing that there was "no contractual relationship" with Augusta National, while at the same time admitting there was no difference between their recognition and treat-ment of the Masters and any other Tour event. This despite pressure from their own sponsors to distance themselves from the con-troversy by taking a principled stand (we had learned this from golf writers who had been at a meeting between Finchem and PGA Tour sponsors). In retrospect, it is not unreasonable to believe that the PGA Tour, in direct contradiction to its written bylaws, had given its tacit approval to Augusta National's hardball tactics by reassuring them that their tournament was not in jeopardy, even before Johnson fired off his by-now-infamous "Point of a Bayonet" press release.

The attraction and power of this club over men at the top (and over the moral imperative of condemning sex discrimination) became clearer still when the sponsors—IBM, Citigroup, Coca-Cola, and General Motors/Cadillac (the official car)—closed ranks against us even *before* we contacted them. In uncannily similar statements that would suggest collusion to a conspiracy theorist, spokespeople for all but Citigroup made a hair-splitting distinction between the Masters Golf Tournament and its host club, Augusta National, in statements to *The New York Times*. They were all variations of this one from IBM: "The Masters and Augusta are separate and we're a sponsor of the Masters . . . we are not a sponsor of Augusta." It was a direct contradiction to statements made about Shoal Creek, when this very same company withdrew sponsorship with the statement "When

> FBR's mission . . . for advancing its business was choreographed with precision targeting of business and financial executives and offers a tutorial on how corporate America extracts value from PGA Tour sponsorships . . . FBR flew in 350 of its employees in waves throughout the week to entertain customers and lay the groundwork for deals . . . The tab for food and entertainment came to $1 million.
>
> Thomas Heath, "Business Links," *The Washington Post*, 2/23/2004, D.1

we learned that this tournament was being played at a club that was exclusionary, we decided it was not an appropriate vehicle for our advertising. *Supporting even indirectly activities which are exclusionary is against IBM's practices and policies* [emphasis added]." Christine Brennan was right. *Acceptable discrimination* versus *unacceptable discrimination* had now been put in writing by one of America's largest corporations.

Despite their attempts to head us off with preemptive statements, we were going forward with plans to contact the sponsors. I ran into Kay Koplovitz, founder of the USA Networks, at a news conference on Capitol Hill. She is the first woman network president in television history, and led the company from 1977 until 1998. USA had been carrying early rounds of the Masters for twenty years. We chatted briefly about the Augusta controversy, and she mentioned that she knew some of the members and might be willing to talk with them. In an e-mail exchange the next day, I told her we were planning polite, private letters to the sponsors, but would also welcome private dialogue with any members. She replied that she would make calls to a couple of members, but they would want to know NCWO's likely actions if they did talk to us: "I don't think they'll walk into a blind," she wrote, "and since you can assume they will imagine only the worst from you, I think it would be best to give my contact a little more on how you'd like to proceed. They are probably afraid of you."

Before I could craft a response, Tiger Woods brought on another media firestorm, this one international, when he was asked about Augusta's membership policy while at the British Open. His tepid reply, "It's one of those things where everyone has . . . they're entitled to set up their own rules the way they want them. It would be nice to see everyone have an equal chance to participate, if they wanted to, but there's nothing you can do about it," sparked a two-inch "HYPOCRITE!" headline in the *New York Post*. Media were all over him because he had run commercials decrying past race discrimination in golf early in his career. "Two-Faced Tiger" was the slogan of the day.

We were besieged with requests to respond to Woods's remark. Because he was the most popular golfer on the planet, we knew better than to attack him directly. On CNN, I merely pointed out that Tiger had a "unique opportunity" to make a difference, but that speaking out against discrimination was the responsibility of all the golfers, not just Woods. It was the truth—but privately I knew he could probably change the Augusta National policy single-handedly if he wanted to. He was the defending Masters champion, he was half-Asian and half–African American, and he enjoyed the highest stature in golf. I was not alone in my thinking. *The New York Times* soon urged him in an editorial to boycott the next Masters, for which they were roundly criticized for "putting all the burden on Tiger" instead of calling on the other golfers to boycott as well.

In retrospect, no one should have been surprised that Woods didn't have a conscience when it came to gender discrimination. His coach, Butch Harmon, was the head pro at the infamously anti-woman Lochinvar in Houston, Texas, where Tiger played quite frequently in the 1990s. Lochinvar didn't even permit women on the grounds to deliver packages, and when a female CNN/Sports Illustrated producer showed up to interview Harmon, she was escorted to the rear entrance of the club. Woods was wearing a shirt with the Lochinvar logo when he won the U.S. Amateur Championship in 1996. Guilt by association? Yes. But he never would have played at or advertised a club that kept out African Americans, even if they created a special exemption for him because he only half-qualified for exclusion.

When I got the time to reply to Kay Koplovitz a few days later, I wrote the following:

. . . this has become an even bigger media circus because of the way Tiger answered when asked the question about women. As I see it, the problem Augusta has now is how to proceed and save face. They should go ahead and invite a woman now and get it behind them; we don't need to be doing a lot of breast beating if they do. We'll just say we're sure they were already on track given the schedule, we're glad they did it, and look forward to other clubs following their lead . . . [but] we will be contacting sponsors and the PGA sooner rather than later, again privately. We are absolutely dedicated to the idea of giving people the opportunity to do the right thing out of the spotlight . . . a discussion with individual members would be productive only if they are internal advocates and can move the process along . . . A private discussion would be strictly private, and we would in no way release any such discussions to the press, or tell the press they were taking place. IF this thing drags on and we get to the point of formal letters to the members who can be identified and asking them for an on the record response, it will be clear that that is what is happening . . . As you know, there are very strong parallels to Shoal Creek here . . . and that is going to become inescapable vis-à-vis the sponsors . . . and corporations identified with members if it continues to be fought in the media.

We held off for another two weeks, in case Koplovitz was successful and it wouldn't be necessary to write the sponsors. Finally word came back from her: "The members aren't going to do anything." So the letters went out, asking the companies to suspend sponsorship of the Masters until Augusta National's discriminatory policy changed. To refute their prior statements to the press that the club and the tournament were separate entities, we provided documentation that the club is organized legally as a for-profit corporation (Augusta National, Inc.), merely "doing business as (DBA)" Augusta National Golf Club and the Masters Golf Tournament.

Once they had a formal letter in hand, the sponsors, except for IBM, became a little more responsive. Only IBM repeated its claim that the club and tournament were separate, and cited ad dollars spent with women's magazines as proof of their commitment to "diversity." When we followed up with a letter citing verbatim their corporate statement about Shoal Creek, they declined to answer. Citigroup's letter also cited magazine awards and "diversity," stating that they were in "dialogue" with the club.

After almost a month, Jeff Dunn, the president of Coca-Cola North America, called me. He said the issue was "firmly in the middle of the desk" of CEO Doug Daft, and they were discussing it with the board (two of their board members, Warren Buffett and Sam Nunn, were among the few known members of Augusta National). Dunn lamented that "everyone," including the other sponsors, was thinking about it and trying to "figure out what to do"—trying to work something out with Hootie Johnson. I got the same message in a telephone conversation with Jeff Coleman, a spokesman from Cadillac, a few days later—but it was delivered in a somewhat more hostile manner. He chastised me for making General Motors give up the sponsorship.

A week or so later we learned from the front page of *The New York Times* that they had indeed "figured out" what to do. In an apparent back-room deal with the sponsors, Hootie Johnson made an announcement that he was "releasing" them. In turn, the companies allowed him to save face by not telling the world that they had been unwilling to continue sponsoring a club that had now become emblematic of sex discrimination. A neat arrangement—Johnson got to give the illusion of control, and the sponsors got off the hook without having to condemn the club so they could return the next year, presumably when the whole thing had blown over.* Their non-statements in response to Johnson's announcement that he was "releasing" the sponsors spoke volumes. Citigroup and General Motors declined to comment, while IBM and Coca-Cola said they respected the club's decision and wished the club well. Not a single sponsor addressed the sex discrimination issue, or gave the slightest public indication that the club's policies were wrong. We were soon to learn that the code of silence on sex discrimination among the boys reached even further, to broadcast television.

When Johnson made his announcement that there would be no sponsors, media attention immediately shifted to CBS,

---

*The Masters went without sponsors until 2005, when IBM returned and SBC and Exxon Mobil were added. Both new sponsors are headed by Augusta National members.

the network that had broadcast the Masters since 1956. Their deal with Augusta National was part of the folklore and mystique of the place. Everyone knew they had a year-to-year contract (some reports even had it as a verbal contract with no written guarantees) and that Augusta dictated the number of commercial minutes CBS could sell per hour—four. The club also had veto power over announcers and even the kind of phrasing that could be used. For example, crowds shouldn't be called a "mob" on the air, but rather "wonderful tournament crowds at Augusta," or similar.[14]

> Loss leaders always reveal the core values of a company, and by airing the commercial-free Masters, CBS demonstrates it is willing to forgo its duty to shareholders in order to uphold the time-honored tradition of elite male privilege . . . And how appropriate that it's in the world of golf that CBS is willing to plant its flag on behalf of the penis prerogative. Golf is what the media masters of the universe play. It's on the fairways that the big boys shmooze and broker deals. It's where the most exclusive power remains and where the huge money moves . . . no wonder CBS/Viacom honchos are willing to lose a million or two in the short run to preserve their spots at the top and on the course.
>
> Jenny Holtz, "Teed-off at CBS," syndicated column, 12/17/2002

Even though CBS had also issued a preemptive statement that they would go ahead with the broadcast without sponsors, NCWO promptly wrote the network, asking them not to broadcast the Masters, pointing out that to do so would legitimize the club's sex discriminatory policy. We had information that the money-losing coverage was already a topic among board members, and that CBS had heard from a lot of viewers that broadcasting the tournament was wrong. The network's response was by now predictable—failure to carry the tournament, they said, would be "a dissservice" to sports fans. Once more the "men's team" had hung together.

Later efforts to influence CBS—including a protest in front of their headquarters by the local NOW chapter and other groups of conscience, as well as a request for a meeting signed by New York City Councilwoman Gail Brewer and Congresswoman Carolyn Maloney—were completely ignored. Even when Thomas Wyman, CBS's former CEO, publicly resigned from the club, calling the members "pigheaded" and backward, the network kept mum.

> CBS doesn't care if it loses money on the Masters broadcast. The company uses Masters week to wine and dine clients that sponsor other shows. They have the CEOs of companies like GM; they have the aerospace industry, communications execs, banks, and credit cards. CBS women are not forbidden to attend, but let's just say they're discouraged. Women clients aren't invited either. And make no mistake, every penny is deducted.
>
> former senior executive at CBS

The stone wall of refusal publicly to decry sex discrimination against women was growing higher, involving more and more men who seemed to have an irrational allegiance to Hootie Johnson and the Augusta National Golf Club. If only we knew who more of the members *were*, there would surely be some who would be willing to denounce the club's practices. Even if they wouldn't do it out of conscience, they surely could not take the negative publicity the memberships would bring down on their companies. If only we knew.

The (Corporate) Good Old Boys Club Exposed

At the time the controversy erupted, Augusta's membership had been secret for the seventy-two years it had been in existence. Only a few selected names were known publicly (Warren Buffett, Sam Nunn, and Lloyd Ward among the most prominent). The full membership roster had been sought by the press (and almost certainly by aspiring members) without success for decades. While reporters were not taking sides publicly, a number were calling NCWO on a regular basis to give suggestions on avenues of investigation to uncover the membership roster. They no doubt believed (correctly, as it turned out) that making the list public would greatly irritate the club, and compel resignations or statements of support for opening the membership to women. Most had tried to get the list themselves, but it was so closely guarded that no more than two or three dozen of the three hundred names were known, and only because they were local to Augusta or connected with the golf business in some way. We had done a little research following the suggested leads, but it was obvious that we didn't have the staffing for the kind of digging it would take. It involved guessing who might be members (out of a list of at least the Fortune 500), combing news reports for any hint that they actually were members, and then trying to verify that. Since one of the hallmarks of membership was the rule against talking to the press or revealing anything the club didn't want public, we knew our chances were pretty slim, and in any case it could take many months, if not years.

At the same time, we were hearing from the public with their own nominations of possible members; some were disgruntled employees or competitors of the suspects. Jack Welch, the retired CEO of General Electric, was identified when his ex-wife blew the whistle on his elaborate lifestyle maintained at the expense of GE stockholders. He had many club memberships, but Augusta National was the only one specifically named during the front-page divorce proceedings.

During the week of the first anniversary of the September 11 attacks on the United States, NCWO removed itself from the press spotlight, announcing that we did not want to speak publicly on the Augusta issue during the time of national commemoration. I was away from the office with my husband for a few days of much-needed rest on our boat. My assistant called, as she did several times each day to go over routine office business. But this time it was more than routine. She told me we had gotten a fax, a list of names divided by state, several pages long, with only the word "Members" at the top. "I don't recognize most of these names," she said. "But Ward and Nunn are on it. It could be the list."

By now I was on a first-name basis with a fair number of reporters, and I talked to many of them every few days. Michael McCarthy, a *USA Today* reporter who covered sports for the Money section of the paper, called a few minutes later. I told him we had gotten a fax that I hadn't seen yet, but it could be the list. He of course wanted it immediately; I told him I had to look at it first and decide what to do. When I saw it, it was obvious that it was the Augusta National roster. The fax number at the top had a Florida area code, and the identified sender LMG Marketing. A web search told us the company didn't exist except as a service business of some kind in New Zealand.

It was also clear that while we now had a list of names by state, the research job to find out who these guys were was still more than we could handle in a timely way. It would take someone with more resources than we had, and someone who would quickly recognize the majority of the names and put them with their companies. After a few days, we devised a plan: We would give it to McCarthy, and give him a head start. He was a Money reporter and we knew these were business leaders, even if we didn't know which guy belonged to which company. *USA Today* would have the resources to research it, but so would some others. So we decided we would fax a few names to *The New York Times, The Atlanta Journal-Constitution,* and ESPN a week later, in case *USA Today* failed to follow through. Since we didn't want anyone to know the list came from NCWO (McCarthy had already agreed not to reveal us as the source) because its authenticity would immediately be questioned, we enlisted a friend in New York, Claire Sargent, to send faxes from a Kinko's. *The New York Times* never got it; their line was continuously busy that day. ESPN obliquely asked me if we faxed them something (I countered with, "What would I know about your fax?") and they dropped it. The *AJC* published a partial list, including mostly the Atlanta area members. We knew then that giving it to McCarthy had been the right choice.

The story broke on September 27, with a big front-page spread in the Sports section and a teaser on A-1 that read

"Secret List Reveals Male Elite" with the Augusta National logo. The story by McCarthy and Erik Brady, which called the club "golf's secret society . . . a golfing version of Yale's Skull and Bones," began with a quote from Boone Knox, a bank executive who said, "We have nothing against women. I love them all. I've got some myself."

The list read like a roster of the Fortune 500 with a member of Congress, some high-level university and charity officials, and powerful statesmen and political brokers thrown in. A select few examples:*

Financial sector: American Express, Bank of America, Citigroup, JPMorgan Chase, Franklin Templeton, Berkshire Hathaway, Morgan Stanley, Prudential

Consumer products: Motorola, Coors, Penske, General Electric, Hormel, Sara Lee, IBM, Alltel, Ford Motor, Microsoft, Bassett Furniture, Milliken, Dan River, Hearst Newspapers, AT&T, Coca-Cola Bottling, ExxonMobil, SBC Communications, Corning Glass, Miller Brewing

Government/Lobbying: U.S. Representative Amo Houghton (R-NY), former Senator Sam Nunn, U.S. Ambassador to Great Britain William Farish, former governor of Georgia Carl Sanders, former Secretary of State George Shultz, former Secretary of Defense Melvin Laird, former Secretary of the Treasury Nicholas Brady (one of his fellow Augusta National members, John Snow, would soon be nominated for Treasury Secretary by President George W. Bush)

---

*A complete list of members and affiliations can be found in the appendix.

Defense contracting: GE, Bechtel, Motorola, Ford, Alltel, IBM, U.S. Steel, AMX, Rockwell International

Charitable/University: Harvard University, University of South Carolina, University of Arkansas, Metropolitan Museum of Art, Memorial Sloan-Kettering Cancer Foundation, Minnesota Museum of American Art, Atlanta Arts Alliance, Carnegie Hall

Interlocking board relationships were pervasive. Sam Nunn, Roger Penske, and Douglas Warner III, former chairman of JPMorgan Chase, were highlighted as on the board of GE, led by CEO Jeffrey Immelt. As chair of GE's compensation committee, Nunn oversaw the golden parachute package of Jack Welch, another Augusta member. Four of the thirteen seats on the JPMorgan Chase board were held by members, and three of Citigroup's board seats, in addition to CEO Sanford Weill. Warren Buffett and Sam Nunn were on Coca-Cola's board (a Masters sponsor) with James Robinson III, former American Express CEO and predecessor to current CEO Kenneth Chenault. Buffett chaired Nunn's Nuclear Threat Initiative advisory board. Shultz headed the International Council of JPMorgan Chase, which was headed by William B. Harrison, New York Stock Exchange board member with soon-to-be NYSE CEO John Reed, himself a former head of Citigroup. It was dizzying.

It was also now clear why the PGA Tour and the United States Golf Association had refused to comply with their own policies against events at discriminatory clubs. Of the five nonplayer members of the PGA Tour policy board, two held Augusta memberships (Richard Ferris, retired CEO of United Airlines, and Charles Knight, CEO of Emerson Electric and IBM director), and a third (Victor Ganzi, CEO of Hearst Corporation) was solidly in the Augusta National camp.* Fred Ridley, USGA vice president, was also a member, as was USGA secretary James Reinhart. USGA committee chair Walter Driver (chairman of King & Spalding, Nunn's firm) would soon become an Augusta member.†

We would later learn that the network of business relationships was much more extensive—*USA Today* had uncovered only the top layer. But even this was more than sufficient to provide a virtual chart of the good old boy network in action.

We thought that at last we had a breakthrough—few corporate executives could afford to be publicly identified with a club that proudly discriminated against women. We believed the exodus would start in the next twenty-four hours, and if enough members spoke out and left the club, the policy would change. Like the race controversy at Shoal Creek a dozen years earlier, the stigma would be too much for customers, stockholders, and employees to tolerate. And had the nation's largest-circulation newspaper "outed" a secret list of corporate CEOs who belonged to a club that barred *minorities,* that's exactly what would have happened. They wouldn't have been able to resign fast enough. But because it was *gender,* the members decided to hang with Hootie Johnson and try to brazen it out. To be fair, a few of them might have believed

---

*I had a conversation with Ganzi at the Gridiron Club dinner in Washington in 2003. He told me that he agreed with the PGA Tour's stand on Augusta, and said, "There is nothing you can do about it." I reminded him that the Tour is a quasi-public entity due to its tax-exempt status, and independent directors like him are specifically charged with representing the public interest. He turned on his heel and walked away.

†Ridley ascended to USGA president in 2004 and still refused to resign his Augusta membership; Driver will likely be the next president.

exposure of the list would change Hootie's mind and they wouldn't have to quit the club. Either way, they kept quiet.

After a few days without a single resignation, we realized the hold of "golf's secret society" on these men was stronger than the internal pressure many were undoubtedly feeling in their companies, and certainly stronger than any moral imperative about fairness to women. No one spoke at all for a week. Then we received a letter from Citigroup, circumspectly worded, that CEO Sanford Weill would "continue to engage in a constructive dialogue on this issue, toward an objective he believes we share with your organization." He was quickly followed by Lloyd Ward, writing on U.S. Olympic Committee stationery, expressing his belief that women should be admitted and stating that he intended to "aggressively" work for that reform. (Ward had not communicated with us previously, despite our having copied him on our original letter to Hootie Johnson.) Next came American Express's Kenneth Chenault, stating that he too was "working from within" to bring about change. Time and events would prove that these were all public relations moves, nothing more.

A few others tried to go on record without saying anything that the club could use against them. U.S. Representative Amo Houghton (R-NY) was officially "neutral," while the U.S. Ambassador to Great Britain was supportive of the goal, but avoided saying he would work toward it. Motorola's chairman said it was up to Hootie to decide. Bank of America also deferred to Johnson, while stating that they were committed to "diversity," had been recognized by *Working Mother* magazine, and had a woman on *Fortune*'s most-powerful list. Ford Motor pointed out that their current CEO was not a member (conveniently failing to mention that their patriarch and board chair was), while one of their former CEOs said women should be members.

Everyone else was silent, silent, silent—except an alarmingly large number of women in the companies on the list. Almost from the first day the list was made public, we started hearing from the women. Women were writing from all over the country telling us their bosses routinely excluded them from business meetings held on the links, and about other ways they were marginalized in the offending corporations. Inside the companies, meetings were held at senior levels, petitions were started, and the topic came up at diversity seminars, management meetings, and stockholder meetings. Female employees felt very strongly that the Augusta National memberships sent the wrong message, hurt their careers, and set the tone for front-line managers in regard to women.

At JPMorgan Chase the women said, "We had a four-hour meeting [with CEO William Harrison] and we couldn't break him." When lower-level women brought it up and started a petition, they were told the CEO's attitude was "get on the boat or get off," but he was not resigning and going forward with the petition could jeopardize their jobs. At Prudential, senior women met with CEO Arthur Ryan and it came up at diversity meetings company wide. Women at Ford Motor told us William Clay Ford's membership was emblematic of wider discrimination within the company that had been covered up for years.[15] Women at American Express said inaction made Chenault's claim to be working from within hollow. Stockholders at Citigroup brought it up at the annual meeting. None of it made any difference. The pull of power had trumped fairness, good business, good sense, personal embarrassment, and even career security in some cases.

Augusta National Member Profile
Sam Nunn, Former Democratic Senator from Georgia

Sam Nunn resigned from the all-male Burning Tree Club in Bethesda, Maryland, in 1990, amid speculation that he was planning to run for president of the United States in 1992. He cited only "personal reasons." In July 2002, a month after the Augusta controversy became news, NCWO and the Golf Channel received a statement from Nunn via fax. The statement, on Nuclear Threat Initiative letterhead (which Nunn chairs), expressed Nunn's confidence that the club would open the membership to women, and if it did not, he was prepared to resign. A few hours later, a memo was faxed on the same letterhead from Cathy Gwin, NTI spokesperson, calling the initial statement "forged." (Did Hootie Johnson slap Nunn down when he got wind of the release, which was leaked prematurely?) Nunn never made another statement about the club or its membership policies.

Nunn did not deny reports that he was one of the Augusta National members entertained by Judge Dudley Bowen at his Bull Haven Ranch outside Augusta, two days after Bowen ruled against NCWO's right to protest outside the front gates of the club.

Nunn joined King & Spalding law firm in Atlanta after leaving the Senate in 1996. King & Spalding is chaired by Walter Driver, another Augusta National member, who is in line to assume leadership of the United States Golf Association in 2006.

Nunn serves on the board of General Electric, where fellow Augusta member Jeffrey Immelt is chair and CEO; fellow members Roger Penske and Douglas Warner III also serve on the GE board. Nunn chairs the compensation committee, which oversees the retirement of former CEO Jack Welch, another Augusta National member.

He is on the board of Coca-Cola with fellow Augusta members Warren Buffett and James D. Robinson III, and he is chair of the Nuclear Threat Initiative; fellow ANGC member Warren Buffett is on this advisory board.

In 2004 the California Public Employees' Retirement System (Calpers), the nation's largest U.S. public pension fund, did not support Nunn's reelection to the Coca-Cola board, stating that his business relationships with Coke could impair objectivity. Calpers also withheld support for Nunn's fellow Augusta members Sanford Weill and Warren Buffett, for the same reason.

Power Will Out

They had served together on corporate boards, on presidential commissions, and on the Business Roundtable. They invested in the same hedge funds and hired each other's children for summer jobs. They even dressed in similar white turtlenecks and khakis. What's more, they'd sponsored each other for memberships in the best clubs. You could see the badges of these interlocking relationships emblazoned on jackets, ties, and belt buckles—the lone cypress of Cypress Point in California, the striped shield of Pine Valley in New Jersey, the Indian chief of Seminole in Florida, the red flag of Augusta National in Georgia . . . Such emblems are akin to a secret handshake . . . golf remains the true communications hub of America's business elite.

Few outsiders have witnessed seven-figure executives lobbying in quiet desperation—often for years—for acceptance into a top-tier club, or observed the Victorian-era rules that govern who can join. Men of power endure this because golf has always been far more than a game. The greatest clubs in the country—Augusta, Oakmont, Pine Valley, Brookline—were founded by businessmen who wanted to establish an inner circle of corporate chieftains and other power brokers. And getting in can be as monumentally hard as being accepted into an elite clique in high school. Bill Gates, the richest man in the world, spent years trying to get into Augusta—and was kept out (until last year) because he had the audacity to say he wanted in.[16]

The power dynamic described here, while it may not be the number one characteristic of men's culture, would certainly rank near the top. Males, much more so than females, are conditioned almost from birth to view the world in terms of hierarchies, power relationships, and being winners. Girls are more often conditioned in the cooperation paradigm with relationships mattering more than personal outcomes in many situations.[17] An interesting example of how this can play out in adult life is provided by a study done in the wake of the Rodney King scandal on how male and female police officers differ in handling suspects who resist arrest. Males are much more likely to view confrontations as "personal challenges," and will "provoke a fight or violence, instead of calming down the situation," making the likelihood of escalation much higher than with female officers.[18]

Law enforcement and professional athletics aside, most of the time the power dynamic between men does not give rise to physical confrontation; it is more likely to be manifested in business hierarchies, money making, attraction of young or beautiful women (*trophy* wives), physical possessions, or in channeled, friendly competitions such as golf or poker.

> An entirely different way of opening a can of whoop-ass.
>
> Advertisement for King Cobra golf driver, *Fortune*, 7/26/2004

We've all heard the saying "He who dies with the most toys wins."

In the business world, many of these toys, or symbols of power, are built into the system, like merit badges in the Boy Scouts. Just like in the Scouts, the badges of power in corporate America change as men get higher up on the power scale. The higher you go, the harder they are to get. In the early days of a career, power could get you an office with a window, later the corner office or the reserved parking space. As the career progresses the badges change; they're now the high-priced car, the $2,000 suit, the right club membership, fatter cigars, better brandy, the bigger expense account, and blonder, younger, thinner women.

As one climbs the corporate hierarchy, the peer group also changes. It becomes more and more differentiated from the population in general. It becomes smaller, ultimately consisting of people outside the company who hold comparable positions. The peer group becomes richer, and *it gathers power at each step*. At the same time, badges that distinguish one individual from everybody else are harder to come by. At the CEO level, corporate jets, unlimited expense accounts, a phalanx of "yes men," and obscenely high salaries and stock options are the norm. Everybody can have anything money can buy. Everybody can swing one more merger, one more acquisition in the corporate arms race for global superiority. Everybody is an alpha male ruling over a different herd.

So how can your average billionaire CEO deal-maker and career breaker wring one more shred of superiority and one-upmanship out of this situation? He gets something money can't buy, that he can't order up on command, and that surely will turn lesser mortals (and lesser business titans) green with envy. That could be something like a highly publicized romance with a young mega–movie star. Or it could be belonging to a golf club that is so exclusive you can't apply for membership. A club surrounded by both mythology and mystique. So exclusive no one knows who the members are—-but everyone knows the members are really at the top of any heap, insiders in the ultimate clique. Golf being the official sport of corporate America and movie stars being hard to come by, since they have their own money and fame and can attract men who don't need Viagra, the club membership moves to the top of the wish list.

And once you've got this thing, this ultimate prize that money can't buy, boy, are you reluctant to give it up. Even if it becomes something of a liability through unenlightened policies and boorish behavior by its leaders; even if it embar-

> I think he was like a kid who had saved his milk money to go to the fair. When the time came, he just couldn't say no, even though the fair was off-limits.
>
> Senior woman at Bank of America on why her boss, CEO Kenneth Lewis, joined Augusta National at the height of the national controversy

rasses your coworkers and your family; even if it threatens the very job that got it for you in the first place, you're afraid to give it up. Not only because you could never get it back, but because it would shame your new set of peers—the other guys who also got this prize (you could say the guys in the *brotherhood*)—into following suit. You would be breaking faith with the team, finking out, acting like a *wuss*.

When groups achieve a certain level of power and influence, sometimes their original purpose is subverted in favor of holding on to the status and the exclusivity that the group has achieved. Status and exclusivity in fact become the raison d'être for both the individual members and the group as a whole—even though the stated purpose (e.g., raising money for charity, supporting the opera, or playing golf) is still the official reason the group exists, and the activities supporting this official purpose continue. But in reality, at this stage the purpose for which the group was formed doesn't much matter—it could have been anything. It's no longer important. What is important is the power and prestige, the influence, the sense that members are not like everybody else—they have reached the top. Within that particular sphere, they are a *power elite*. And power elites would not be human if they didn't enjoy their place and want not only to keep it, but to strengthen it where possible. And if the power sphere happens to be business related and male dominated, that's where the problem comes in for working women.

> It's a lost cause with him. He'll never do it alone. He said if any of his friends would do it, he would. I have made arguments to him about being a leader. But he won't listen. He just doesn't have [the courage].
>
> Senior woman at JPMorgan Chase, on hearing that a large group of socially responsible investment firms had asked her boss, William B. Harrison, to resign from Augusta National because the membership sent the wrong message to stockholders, customers, and employees

The power dynamic manifests itself in a number of ways.

Power re-creates itself in its own image. Psychologists have long known that we're most comfortable with people who are like us, both in appearance and ways of thinking. It has been well documented that managers like to hire people who look like themselves. In most of corporate America, that still means white and male. That's why laws against employment discrimination were passed in the first place—women and minority men just weren't on the radar screens of the folks doing the hiring and promoting. The so-called "neutral" processes in corporations were firmly enforcing a white male quota system. That is still true—most companies have "diversity" in management only to the extent that it does not threaten the traditional (some would even say *natural*) balance.

Despite claims by some that women and minority men have taken all the jobs, the results of this re-creation process are fairly easy to see, even from casual observation. The numbers speak for themselves—and the higher you go in the hierarchy, the greater the enforcement of traditional quotas in favor of the dominant group. In most companies, there will be a fair number of women and minority men in the rank and file, fewer at lower management, and still fewer at middle management. At the very top level of the Fortune 500, there are only eight female CEOs. Even in companies like Citigroup, where *women* are a 56 percent majority overall, *men* hold 56 percent of the "officials and managers" jobs. There is only one female top executive. She is paid 50 percent of the average for men at her level.[19]

Power elites enforce norms and systems that guarantee continued power. At the highest levels of business, the board of directors is a major enforcer of the status quo—both in its own makeup and that of the top management of the company.

Consider what happens when an individual is chosen to be on a corporate board for the first time. He (or in rare cases, she) is usually nominated by the CEO or someone already on the board, and brought into a new environment with its own culture and skill set. The nominator has an interest in seeing this individual succeed, as it will reflect well on his judgment and business acumen. The newcomer, at the same time, wants to

> . . . boards of directors are notoriously social organizations, where the goal is not to maximize profits but to avoid personal embarrassment while maintaining social cohesion within the board and the larger corporate community . . . it is simply bad form to nitpick over a couple of million dollars with another member of the club . . .
>
> Steven Pearlstein, "A Rigged Market for CEO," *The Washington Post,* 4/30/2003, E.1

belong, wants to overcome any notion that he is unworthy or an impostor. So the new member is "trained" through mentoring and role modeling, quickly picking up on the board culture and the behavior and knowledge necessary to succeed. That means the new recruit must be *assimilated* into the environment, in turn becoming a likely candidate for long-term tenure and nomination for more boards. If the environment is one of exclusion of certain groups, or one that traditionally has enforced an unwritten quota limiting certain groups, it is not hard for the new individual to figure out what is expected. Boat rockers don't last as board members. So for a person in the minority (a woman or a man of color) there is actually a disincentive to advocate bringing others like themselves into the circle, as they are likely to be accused of "pushing an agenda" and not behaving like a "team player." And we all know what happens to team members who don't function as they're expected to function. They're cut.

The system is self-perpetuating. It is not uncommon to see individuals (white men as well as "token" females and minority males) sitting on several boards, since these individuals have shown they have the skills necessary for board membership, and they have internalized the unspoken rules about acceptable board composition. While one individual can certainly make changes, the probability of success is much higher if that individual is part of the majority, and one of those with the most power. These majoritarians are, of course, the most comfortable (and have the best developed sense of entitlement) and therefore they have the least incentive to let others unlike themselves into the circle. They are unlikely to even see the need for it, so long as the quotas are covered. This process is exactly how *systemic barriers* are created and maintained.

The board example has obvious parallels in other settings where the dynamics of exclusivity, exclusion, and entitlement converge to produce power elites that are extremely resistant to change: settings like corporate executive suites and their outdoor annexes such as Augusta National Golf Club.

There are other ways that elites enforce their power at a systemic level. Consider tax breaks for corporations. A few states have laws that disallow tax deductions for money spent at discriminatory clubs. But the federal law does not, so corporate titans taking the company plane for a round at Augusta or entertaining clients to the tune of a million dollars a week during the Masters can do it on the taxpayers' dime, and legally at that. If these expenses weren't deductible, the company wouldn't stand for them. But the same power elites on the golf course have

> Golf and business often go hand in hand. Travelers Group Inc. Chairman Sandy Weill quipped at a news conference in New York last year that he and Citicorp CEO John Reed had worked hard to complete an agreement to merge the two companies for $76.4 billion by the first week in April—so Weill could go to Augusta and wine and dine 130 guests.
>
> "Golf, Business Go Hand in Hand: Masters Attracts Big Hitters," *The Times-Picayune*, 4/4/1999

power lobbyists in Washington to persuade the Congress to vote in their best interests—it keeps things neat. (The citizens of Buffalo, New York, got a double whammy, it turns out. Their congressman, Amo Houghton, who retired in 2004, was a member of Augusta National, so his buddies could just bypass their lobbyists and talk to him directly while on the links.)

Power creates a sense of entitlement. Most men at some level know that maleness is valued over femaleness in the culture, and we are all taught in subtle ways that males have first claim on jobs, sports, and opportunities. (This does not differ in minority communities. Women of color are the first to admit their brothers are sexist too.) But for the ordinary man the cultural valuation of all things male does not translate into the sense of super-entitlement that corporate power elites exhibit. That comes from somewhere else—a corporate system that has evolved to the point where value is placed on its leaders that is far out of proportion to their actual worth.

Consider CEO pay. In 2003 the average CEO pay in large companies was more than three hundred times that of the average worker (up from 42:1 in 1982). The rise in compensation for the top dogs outstripped rises in inflation, profits, and the S&P 500. Conservative economist Robert Samuelson had this to say:

> The scandal of CEO pay is not that it ascended to stratospheric levels . . . [but that] so few CEOs have publicly raised their voices in criticism or rebuke . . . there's a widespread self-serving silence. If they can't defend what they're doing, then maybe what they're doing is indefensible . . .

Sprinkling so much money over so few people has created a sense of entitlement . . . What this produces is a self-justifying set of rules and practices, reinforced by a growing insensitivity to appearances.[20]

The reader will recognize immediately that these words could as easily have applied to the controversy over membership in Augusta National Golf Club. CEOs did not raise their voices against the club's exclusion of women; there was a conspiracy of self-serving silence. It was obvious they believed themselves exempt from society's standards against discrimination, immune to criticism from the public or discipline from their companies, even in the face of employee unrest and questions at stockholder meetings.

Power creates invulnerability, leading to a flaunting of society's standards. As individuals become more powerful, whether it's in politics, business, sports, or some other area like head of a prestigious golf club, they are increasingly surrounded by others whose job (or golf memberships) they control and who tell them how clever,

> Behind his back they were all calling him an idiot. To his face they told him how right he was.
>
> Reporter on how members treated Hootie Johnson over his handling of the controversy surrounding admitting women

smart, and right they are. In business and politics this insulating layer is usually composed of lawyers and accountants to smooth over those little scrapes with the SEC, the FEC, or ethics committees. In entertainment and sports, the insulation is also composed of public relations people to put a positive spin on the latest barroom brawl, cocaine charge, rape, or child molestation. Sometimes exemptions from standards that apply to others are put in writing. Consider this from American Express's instructions for employees on upholding the company ideals in their behavior:

> **Q:** If, as employees, we must decline invitations from suppliers, customers or others for an event, resort or other function that might seem extravagant or unrelated to business, then why are certain senior officers of the Company allowed to accept invitations to attend [such] events . . . ?

> **A:** Occasionally, the Company identifies opportunities to enhance or maintain important business relationships through attendance at more elaborate functions. Senior officers of the Company may be permitted and, in fact, encouraged to attend because of their relationships with significant customers and suppliers, which are important to the Company's business. At the same time, the Company considers carefully which kinds of functions are appropriate and authorizes attendance only when important business relationships are at stake.

So you see, the rich really are different.

Power elites are also increasingly insulated from the sanctions that ordinary people are subject to when they misbehave. With more concentrated power comes

> Rigas and two of his offspring face criminal charges that they looted Adelphia Communications to pay for a golf course and other personal expenditures.[21]
>
> Carrie Johnson, "Trial Against Adelphia Executives to Open," *The Washington Post*, 2/23/2004, A.5

an enhanced sense of that entitlement, which men (and a very few Martha Stewarts) have been inculcated with in the first place, leading, not without justification, to a sense of invulnerability. The belief

> Other accounting tricks were more complex, the indictment alleges, including a deal known as Project Grayhawk, after an Arizona golf resort where Enron executives met.
>
> "Ex-CEO Turns Himself In," Carrie Johnson, *The Washington Post*, 2/20/2004, A.10

that if you're powerful the normal rules in society don't really apply is validated by your surroundings. In fact, breaking the rules to get where you are is excused as nothing more than hard-nosed business, shrewd politics, or the result of occupational pressure. We've seen this again and again as sports and entertainment figures get a pass on cocaine possession or beating up their girlfriends, politicians get a pass on dallying with interns or taking "contributions" that result in big government contracts, and executives who lose billions and squander the retirements of thousands of workers get a slap on the wrist as they jump out of harm's way with the aid of their golden parachutes.

We've all heard the saying "Power corrupts, and absolute power corrupts absolutely." To that we might add, *Loyalty to power overshadows other loyalties, including gender and race.* Statistics show that when it comes to income, black men gain more from being male than they lose from being black, particularly at high levels.[22] It is also well known in business that after women reach a certain level, they are less likely to want to help other women advance. Two dynamics are likely at work here. As association with a certain group conveys more power, individuals begin to identify more with that group and less with

> The subject that clammed [Fortune 500 CEOs] up the tightest was what they called the "Augusta issue." Talking about the fact that some exclusive clubs exclude women as members—Augusta National in particular—was akin to a *Sopranos* family capo talking to the feds.
>
> *Fortune*, April 14, 2003, p. 168

other groups to which they belong. They also seek personal validation by the power group (almost everyone feels like an impostor at some level—women more so than men). In the business world this means behaving like the others. Holding on to the power—and gaining more of it—inevitably becomes more important than loyalty to what is now a less important group. Since the power group in corporate America is still overwhelmingly male and white, the less important group in the woman executive's case is other women, and in the minority male's case, others of his race or ethnicity.

In the majority male's case, however, the power group aligns perfectly with his race and gender group. So these loyalties, far from being lessened, are actually reinforced. He doesn't have to make a choice between his race and/or gender group and the power elite—he doesn't even have to think about it. When he promotes a member of his group up the executive ranks, or proposes a new board member who is not only like him but like the majority, he is never accused of "pushing an agenda." His candidate's credentials are never questioned because the nomination may be the result of a "special interest" mentality. In fact, it's the opposite; his nomination is seen as merely "normal." So not only is his choice reinforced, but *his entitlement to make that particular choice* is reinforced through the tacit acceptance on the part of others that the board seat is going to one of its rightful owners.

A stark example of allegiance to power over one's other reference groups surfaced in the Augusta National controversy with American Express CEO Kenneth Chenault and USOC head Lloyd Ward, two of the four known African-American members of the club. When the Ku Klux Klan publicly announced its support for Augusta's policies, stating that they would demonstrate in favor of the club because "this equal rights stuff has gone too far," both men were conspicuously silent. Equally telling, Tiger Woods, who had appeared in commercials decrying race discrimination in golf, refused to denounce the Klan's support, merely saying, "If it's not the thing [about the controversy], it's another."

Power trumps fairness and in some cases honesty and integrity. One of the reasons NCWO wrote to Augusta National about the exclusion of women in the first place was that we believed our support would help Lloyd Ward make change from the inside, as he had told Christine Brennan he was committed to doing. Though we copied him on our original correspondence to the club, he never responded to us until the full membership list was "outed" five months later. Ward was put in a bind when a couple of other CEOs

> I like Lloyd, but he cannot change [Augusta] from the inside. I don't think you would join the Klan and try to change it from the inside.
>
> Herb Perez, USOC executive committee Michael Bamberger and Lester Munson, "A Mole in Hootie's Midst?" *Sports Illustrated*, 10/21/2002, p. 22

(in what turned out to be purely public relations moves) expressed support for change after the negative publicity hit. Ward's letter expressed his intent to "aggressively" work for reform. The initial publicity had put Ward on the spot with the USOC executive committee because he had failed to disclose his membership when he was hired. Now some of his bosses were calling on him to make a choice between his job and Augusta National.

A month later, Ward was already starting to backtrack on his promises, saying in a news conference that "I can't change Augusta; Augusta has to change itself." Members of the U.S. Senate Commerce, Science and Transportation Committee, which oversees the USOC, were furious with Ward over his membership. Both Senator Barbara Boxer (D-CA) and Senator Ben Nighthorse Campbell (R-CO) asked him about it during hearings on unrelated ethics code violations. (Well, they might not have been unrelated. Ward was accused of steering Olympic business to his brother. The question was asked more than once whether the accusations came to light because Billy Payne, fellow Augusta member and CEO of the Atlanta Committee for the Olympic Games, wanted to punish Ward for speaking out on Augusta in the first place.) Ward capitulated to the club and rendered his earlier pledges to work for women's acceptance meaningless when he told the senators: "Augusta is a great institution . . . Augusta isn't going to change based on my resignation." In the end, Ward resigned his USOC position. The press speculated that he needed the Augusta National membership to network for his next job.

Group loyalty combined with power can trump good judgment and override individual moral codes. All Americans, male and female, are inculcated with a strong value for loyalty to one's group. In the great majority of cases, group loyalty is a good thing. It fosters team spirit for athletics, cohesiveness in military units, productivity in business, and dedication to the public good in community service organizations. But most of us know "loyalty" is perverted when it serves a purpose counter to society's values. While we might stay in a group even if it occasionally took a stand we disagreed with, we wouldn't remain if the group stood for something society condemns (like discrimination) or if it conspired to break the law by systematically stealing employee pension funds with accounting scams and bogus companies designed to hide losses and irregularities.

And at the extremes, group loyalty can go terribly wrong. It can facilitate lawlessness under the cover of secrecy and lead to group actions and cover-ups of those actions that group members would never consider as individuals. Examples can range from illegal accounting schemes to harmful and sometimes fatal hazing by fraternity brothers, to gang rapes (too often by athletic team members), military atrocities, and terrorism. It is probably no accident that most of the excesses we learn about from such action occur in male-dominated or exclusively male groups. It likely stems from a combination of factors: more exposure to conditioning by the culture, more power (both physical power and that derived from being a member of the dominant group), and to a lesser degree the sense of entitlement and invulnerability that comes from power.

> Investigators are exploring whether Dennis Kozlowski, ex-CEO of Tyco International, who is accused of illegally obtaining $600 million in company funds, used some of the money to help fund his golf interests. Kozlowski is a founding member of the GC [golf club] of New England . . . featuring a $65,000 membership fee. Prosecutors suspect he may have used some of the purloined Tyco money to fund his stake in the venture.[23]
>
> *Golfdigest.com*, 10/11/2002

Obviously the average man does not participate in illegal, immoral, or harmful group actions. But the average man (much more so than the average woman) has been exposed, again and again, to the code of loyalty to a group that can lead to actions that are not in his best interests, nor in the best interests of society. It's about living in a culture that links masculinity to power, dominance, and control. In everyday life it might never affect most, because they're not faced with the stark choice of taking a stand and doing what's right versus betraying an unspoken loyalty oath to the "brotherhood of men." But depending on the circumstances, if he is faced with such a choice, the same average guy might look the other way or think long and hard about what to do before making the moral choice.

Women encounter these situations too—it's just that they have not been conditioned to group allegiance in the same way, or to the same degree, that men have. It is also very rare that we hear of group actions by women that are comparable to fraternity hazings or gang rapes. But not necessarily because women are genetically predisposed to being kinder and gentler human beings, as many would argue. If women had had the same power, status, and conditioning that men have had over the centuries, we might see parallels in female group behavior. But these "antecedent conditions" have not existed historically, and they still don't exist, even in the most advanced societies. So we'll have to leave the genetic arguments to another planet or to another ten millennia in the future.

Augusta National Member Profile
Arthur F. Ryan, chair, CEO, and president, Prudential Financial

Arthur Ryan has been chairman and chief executive officer of Prudential since 1994. A letter bearing his signature in the front of the company's diversity brochure reads:

> We require that each leader in our company play a critical role in creating an environment where every employee has an opportunity to succeed and where diversity is respected and sought after in our business dealings.

Ryan serves on the Committee to Encourage Corporate Philanthropy (CECP) with fifteen other Augusta National members, including Warren Buffett, Sanford Weill, Kenneth Lewis, and Philip Purcell. After the roster was made public, Ryan's Augusta membership became a topic within the company. Several senior women sent him a letter expressing their belief that he should resign for the good of the firm, and it was discussed around water coolers and in human resource meetings.

After nine months (well past the 2003 Masters) Ryan agreed to meet with a select group who wanted to air their concerns. The women armed themselves with background material, including Augusta National's press release, correspondence with NCWO, and a Harvard Business Review case that advised any responsible company to stay away from discriminatory venues.

"The meeting went decently. He was not combative, and was interested in our perspective," said one participant. Still, Ryan had "no timetable in his head" for resigning, even though he said he might consider it. "We gave him all the arguments, including that he wouldn't be a member of the club if the issue was race," the woman continued. "He said it was a personal membership, all the while acknowledging that it was his position that got him there. If any of his friends would [resign] then he would." They implored him to talk to other Augusta National members and do some kind of joint announcement.

At the same time, it was known in the company that Ryan was in line for a national "good guy" award from a large, well-established women's group, but the Augusta membership was a stumbling block. He was still giving lip service to the idea of working for internal change, even though the scandal was now more than a year old and the club had recently hardened its position by announcing that it would "never" admit a woman.

Ryan would have to address the concerns of his female employees before the award could go forward. A plan was crafted by the public relations and legal departments for him to sign an internal letter to the women of his company expressing his intention to resign from the club if the membership did not open in a reasonable length of time. The plan would be acceptable to the women, the company officials who drafted the letter were satisfied with it, and the awarding organization had signed off on it. Following the suggestion made in the initial meeting, Ryan had made calls to Weill and Chenault, and he "did not get any support" for a plan to address the problem with or without other Augusta National members, according to the women.

In the end, the letter lay on his desk, and he would not sign it. The award was never conferred. Almost three years after the situation surfaced, Ryan's female employees are still waiting for him to show some leadership on a matter they termed "morally reprehensible" when they first met with him.

Buying a Pass:
Our Record Is Good on Race,
Isn't That Enough?

The dynamics of race were prominent at many levels in the Augusta controversy. From the beginning, the club touted Hootie Johnson's credentials as a civil rights leader. The fact that he had served on the National Urban League board (with Vernon Jordan, who is *black*) was repeated endlessly on the radio and in print. He had supported an African-American man for Congress and worked on a plan to desegregate South Carolina's colleges in 1968 after three civil rights protesters were killed by state troopers. It was clear that in Johnson's mind, having a decent record on race issues gave him a pass when it came to other forms of prejudice—most notably bias against women. It was less clear why more editors didn't question this logic, and why sympathetically showcasing someone who championed blatant sex discrimination was acceptable, when they would never profile an unrepentant racist in the same way.

The fact that the club has a racist past was downplayed, or mentioned only in passing, usually in the context of its opening to black men in the wake of the Shoal Creek contro-

> When I first went to Augusta in 1962, I volunteered to serve as a traffic and crowd controller along with several hundred other soldiers. At that time, the Masters used U.S. Army soldiers to control the crowds with ropes and it was a good opportunity to see the golf tournament. To my surprise, I was told that Black Soldiers could not be used in that capacity at Augusta Golf Club . . . let me know if you need a passenger to ride on the buses to Augusta.
>
> Harold Looney, letter to NCWO, 11/17/2002

versy (according to one reporter, they had opened to black men only after "being pistol-whipped by the PGA Tour behind closed doors" after Shoal Creek). In fact, the club's racist record was a good deal deeper than its failure to invite an African-American member until forced. Blacks weren't barred from Augusta National—they were the servants and caddies in a strictly maintained racial divide. Members and players were always white, caddies and servants were always black. The club maintained a strict rule that only black caddies served the players until 1983, when professional players who had their own caddies were allowed to bring them to the Masters. *The New York Times* put it this way: "All those black caddies also were part of the image that Augusta National projected, knowingly or not, as America's last plantation with the caddie yard over there in the pine trees beyond the delivery driveway. In the sprawling white clubhouse, the wealthy Augusta National members in their green jackets still are served by black waiters, black bartenders and black locker-room attendants."[24]

Even more damning, at one time in its history the club shamelessly exploited its black employees for entertainment. "Battle Royals" were held: boxing matches with five black men in the ring at once, all blindfolded, "as a diversion for Augusta National members." The last man standing was declared the winner.[25]

Though Augusta National was now past its race problem at least on the surface, Johnson openly made the case that sex discrimination was not comparable to race discrimination in an interview he granted to select members of the press in November 2002:

> Racial discrimination and gender are two different things. Do you know of any constitutional lawyer that's ever said they were the same? Do you know any civil rights activists that said it was the same? Do you? It's not relevant. Nobody accepts them as being the same.[26]

Johnson was right about one thing. Some people, most notably his corporate sponsors and CEO members, apparently didn't see the two forms of discrimination as the same. Reinforcing Brennan's original observation that some sex discrimination is still acceptable, corporate leaders refused to speak up, even though the NAACP, the Southern Christian Leadership Conference, and Rainbow/PUSH had denounced the club publicly. Neither would other golfers speak up after Lee Elder, the first black to play in the Masters, Lee Trevino, and South African golf legend Gary Player condemned the all-male policy. When Tiger Woods refused to take a principled stand, he was roundly criticized

> And Tiger Woods disgusts me with his "I'm only one person" attitude. Rosa Parks was only one person. I've got news for Tiger Woods. He isn't half the man Rosa Parks was!
>
> Fax to NCWO, Los Angeles, 11/13/2002

in the press, since he had run television commercials early in his career condemning race discrimination in golf.

Of course, NCWO consistently pointed out that sex and race discrimination are indeed comparable, the spelling is just different. Our strongest spokespersons were African-American women, including C. DeLores Tucker of the National Congress of Black Women, Jackie Woods of the American Association of University Women, and civil rights icon Dr. Dorothy Height. Dr. Jane Smith, CEO of Business and Professional Women/USA, minced no words when asked how she could denounce Augusta National when she herself was a graduate of Spelman College, a traditionally black all-female institution in Atlanta. "Spelman was founded to create opportunity where none existed," she said, "not to deny opportunity. If places like Augusta National and its predecessors did not exist to bar the doors to women and minorities, there would have been no need for a Spelman." Janice Mathis, vice president of Rainbow/PUSH, put it another way: "I have been a black woman all my life. And I have never been able to tell the difference when I have been discriminated against because I am black, or because I am a woman. It feels the same either way."

Still, Hootie's statement resonated with many people, mostly men but a few women as well. They just didn't get it, and they didn't even know why they didn't get it. Sex discrimination *didn't* seem as serious. The legal and cultural history of our country tells us a lot about why.

Johnson's assertion that constitutional lawyers would not equate sex and race discrimination, when taken in a narrow legal context, was technically correct for much of our history. The roots of that technical correctness tell us a lot about why Americans, many of good will, have been taught by the lawmakers, the culture, and the courts not to put sex discrimination on the same level of seriousness or moral repugnance as race discrimination. Historically, antidiscrimination laws were first crafted to remedy discrimination against nonwhite males, while leaving sex discrimination unaddressed. Most of the laws against sex discrimination at the federal level have parentage elsewhere—they were modeled after, or became a part of, similar laws meant to remedy some other wrong, such as labor rights or race discrimination. And that's where the problem comes in.

When the Constitution was crafted, the ruling class was white, male, and land-owning. Rights of full citizenship were conferred on that basis. "Persons" granted citizenship were understood to be white and male, but the framers could not agree on whether land ownership should also be a requirement for voting. Unable to resolve this issue, they left voting requirements to the states.

The Fourteenth Amendment, ratified three years after the abolition of slavery in 1868, granted citizenship to "persons born or naturalized in the United States," and the right to vote to nonwhite men, but not to women. It also guaranteed "equal protection under the law" for all "persons." The breathtaking hypocrisy of the state proposing a constitutional amendment guaranteeing equal protection for all citizens while explicitly denying the female half the vote was not lost on the suffragists. Controversy raged in the years before adoption as to whether women should be included, with the formidable Susan B. Anthony on the side of women (black and white), and the equally formidable Frederick Douglass against. The influential newspaper editor Horace Greeley summed up Douglass's arguments when he admonished the suffragists as such:

. . . hold your claims, though just and imperative, . . . in abeyance until the negro is safe beyond peradventure, and your turn will come next. I conjure you to remember that this is "the negro's hour," and your first duty now is to go through the State and plead his claims.[27]

It went without saying that he meant *male* Negroes.

Ultimately the guys prevailed (surprise!), introducing the word "male" into the Constitution for the first time, and enshrining in the Constitution that race discrimination was more serious than sex discrimination. Women would have to work another fifty-two years to pass a separate amendment just to gain equal voting rights (at that time women were also denied the right to own property, the right to divorce, to child custody, to their own earnings, and to attend college, and husbands could legally rape and beat their wives). Cementing the notion that the equal protection clause really meant equal protection of black men, for the next one hundred years courts ruled against women seeking equal treatment under the Fourteenth Amendment, beginning with Anthony's trial for voting illegally in 1873.[28]

Not until 1971 would the Supreme Court find a law discriminating against women unconstitutional under the Fourteenth Amendment. Then-professor Ruth Bader Ginsburg brought the case on behalf of a woman denied equal footing with her husband in the settlement of an estate under Idaho law, which declared that "males must be preferred to females," in estate administration.[29] Though a separate Equal Rights Amendment for women was introduced in Congress in 1983, it failed to be ratified by the thirty-eight required states, despite a national ratification drive by feminists from 1972 to 1982.

With the Constitution affording little help to women, specific statutes had to be crafted to combat discrimination item by item. And not all have helped. Up until the 1960s, laws "protecting" women in the workplace were the norm, with forty-odd states having statutes limiting the number of hours, duties, or the times of day women could work. So-called protective legislation had the unintended (or not so unintended) consequence of devaluing women as workers, further reinforcing justifications for job segregation and unequal pay scales.

At the same time, while black males were not officially barred from most jobs, they were unofficially shut out because of their race. States tackled this problem long before the federal government acted in 1964, and the relegation of sex discrimination as a "lesser" form of discrimination is rooted in these state laws as well as in the way the Fourteenth Amendment was written and interpreted. New York's 1945 fair employment statute, which became the prototype for laws in other states, created a state agency to eliminate discrimination "because of race, creed, color, or national origin." No mention was made of sex. Sex discrimination was thought of as "normal."

This remained true throughout the civil rights movement that began with the Montgomery bus boycott in 1955. Though women worked in the movement, it was led by men and seen primarily, even by many within it, as a movement to establish the equal personhood of black men.

> My dad taught us growing up that no man was any better than any other man.
>
> Jesse Epps, a leader of the civil rights movement's "I Am a Man" campaign in 1968. From "I Am a Man," essay in *My Soul Looks Back in Wonder,* Juan Williams, AARP/Sterling, 2004

Indeed, "I Am a Man" was one of the most frequently used slogans for placards on picket lines, and remains one of the most enduring images of the era. Only one woman, Dr. Dorothy Height, was in the inner-circle "group of eight" leaders of the civil rights movement in the 1960s. The 1963 march on Washington, culminating in Dr. Martin Luther King Jr.'s "I Have a Dream" speech at the Lincoln Memorial, explicitly excluded women speakers over her objections. According to Dr. Height, "That movement was vital to awakening the women's movement . . . [men] were happy to include women in the human family, but there was no question as to who headed the household!"[30]

So the civil rights movement, powerful as it was in permanently instilling in the American psyche the notion that race discrimination is morally wrong, had virtually no effect on attitudes about sex discrimination. In fact, one could make the argument that the civil rights movement's success resulted in the equating of *discrimination* with *race discrimination only* in the American consciousness. At the least, it had the effect of once again elevating race discrimination to a higher level of seriousness than sex discrimination.

A telling incident on the culture of discrimination is illustrated by the founding of the Federal City Club in Washington, D.C., in 1963. The Kennedys were in the White House—Bobby Kennedy was attorney general. A black man, George Weaver, had been given a federal appointment in the Labor Department, unusual at the time. Weaver was taken to lunch at the exclusive Metropolitan Club by his predecessor. The lunch went without incident, but a few days later the host received a letter from the Metropolitan informing him that blacks were not allowed. An outraged Bobby withdrew his pending nomination for membership and decided to form another club—it would be called the Federal City Club—where blacks would be welcomed.

Well, not all blacks—just the male half.[31]

Federal City, like the Metropolitan and their tony cousin The Cosmos Club, was all male. Gender was not mentioned, and apparently not thought about. "It never occurred to us," said James Symington, a founding member.[32] "The only criteria was 'demonstrable interest in public affairs' but the idea of women just didn't cross our minds."* Roxanne Roberts, who wrote about the founding of Federal City forty years later, put it this way: "The idea of discrimination based on race seemed wrong, but gender discrimination seemed reasonable."[33]

Laws followed public opinion. President Lyndon Johnson, a Texan who had known racist society firsthand, pushed the Civil Rights Act of 1964 through Congress. That women also gained employment rights under Title VII of the law was, literally, a joke. The Labor Department had submitted data to Congress showing widespread employment discrimination against African Americans, whose unemployment rate was more than double that of whites. Wage rates for white versus nonwhite workers of both genders were submitted (men compared to men, women to women), along with data showing that white women made half the wages of white men, and nonwhite women made only 24.8 percent when compared to the highest wage standard, white men. But the gender data

---

*Ironically, when asked at a Congressional hearing in 2002 why he did not disclose his membership in Augusta National to the U.S. Olympic Committee when he was applying for the CEO position (in light of the USOC's mission of gender equality), Lloyd Ward echoed Symington's words: "I had no perspective on why that would be important. It was just not an issue."

were simply ignored by the committee, as evidenced in the Republican statement:

> Aside from the political and economic considerations . . . we believe in the creation of job equality because it is the right thing to do. We believe in the inherent dignity of man. He is born with certain inalienable rights. His uniqueness is such that we refuse to treat him as if his rights . . . are bargainable. All vestiges of inequality *based on race* must be removed . . . [emphasis added]

Now, here's the joke. Southerners were opposed to the bill and wanted to kill it at all costs. So Representative Howard Smith of Virginia thought of a foolproof plan: Include sex. Reasoning that the *addition of protections for women would be seen as both silly and radical,* he figured he had provided colleagues with the perfect excuse for voting against the bill without seeming racist. Ultimately the joke was on Smith, because the bill passed.[34] Title VII prohibited discrimination in employment based on sex, race, color, religion, and national origin.

Significantly, women were left out of Title II, the portion of the law dealing with public accommodations. This omission perpetuated the notion that sex discrimination didn't need to be addressed in the same way as race discrimination, and that keeping women out of certain places (including colleges and universities, law schools, and medical schools) merely because they were women was acceptable and "normal." The omission in education was remedied with Title IX of the Education Amendments of 1972, but the public accommodations law still does not include sex. This is why women are still fighting at state and local levels, under a hodgepodge of laws, to gain admission to "private" clubs that are de facto public accommodations, serving as virtual recruitment salons for top executives.

There is no question that the second-class history of sex discrimination in the evolution of antidiscrimination law, combined with a weaker cultural prohibition against gender bias, continues to affect outcomes for women, particularly in the workplace. What lawyers call the *level of scrutiny* by the courts in sex discrimination cases was historically lower than that for race. Translation: Courts have been slower to recognize sex discrimination and have taken it less seriously, even when the letter of the law is explicit.

But while Hootie Johnson was technically correct (probably without knowing it) that legal histories differ for sex and race discrimination, what the government treated as "legal" in the past can be a mighty poor substitution for "right" in the here and now. In the case of discrimination, there's a pretty simple test. Anytime you hear arguments defending sex discrimination, ask yourself these questions: Would this person be making this argument if the subject was race? And if they did, would I accept that argument? If the CEOs of some of America's largest companies stood together and said, "There is nothing wrong with a little race discrimination," would we think maybe they were right or at least give them the benefit of the doubt? Of course not. And that's exactly what they did when they hid in silent solidarity behind Hootie and let him make the argument about women.

Even when the Ku Klux Klan came out in support of the club's sex discrimination, neither the club leadership nor its individual corporate members denounced their white-hooded supporters. On the day of the KKK's announcement ("They have the right to exclude anyone they want"), the club tried to blame the KKK support on NCWO with this statement: "As a result of the controversy created by political activists, a number of organizations, some of them extreme, have sought to voice their political views . . . For our critics to try to capitalize on this sideshow is utterly reprehensible and has no place in any civilized discourse." Nowhere did they name or condemn the KKK, or specifically reject its support. In the weeks following, they did succeed in planting the idea with the press that the KKK was really involved only to oppose Jesse Jackson, not support Augusta National. Almost all of the reporting reflected this change by the day of NCWO's protest a couple of months later at the Masters Tournament—the Klan was widely characterized as in attendance to counter Jackson's Rainbow/PUSH.

At the same time Augusta National was making the case that there was no parallel between race and gender discrimination, they were borrowing anti–civil rights rhetoric and actions right out of the 1960s. The mayor of Augusta, Bob Young, helped them along in an interview on *Real Sports with Bryant Gumbel,* broadcast on national television:

G: How concerned are you, Mr. Mayor, about the extent to which what happens [tournament week] will impact the way the city of Augusta is viewed by America?

Y: Yes, it's going to be very important. It's going to be critical to us.

G: How would you characterize the community's attitude toward those who will be coming down here for the tournament for the first time, for the sole purpose of protesting?

Y: I would suspect they would be viewed as a bunch of out-siders who come in here to stir up trouble.

G: You realize to a lot of people that smacks of the same kind of talk we heard in the early sixties, only of a racial bent?

Y: Well, yeah. You could say that. Sure.

G: Would you allow that a protest that goes unseen and unheard by those who it's intended to influence is no protest at all?

Y: That has some merit, and maybe that's the best scenario in this case.

Two months before the Masters Tournament, the Augusta-Richmond County Commission started to revamp the city ordinances to make it impossible for NCWO to mount a protest in front of the club. The new law would give sole discretion over the permit process to the Richmond County Sheriff, Ronnie Strength, and declare that a group as small as five persons needed a permit to assemble. The sheriff would also have sole discretion over protest location and time, and the permits had to be applied for twenty days before a planned action.

It took three tries to change the ordinance. The ten-member commission was all male, with five black members and five white members. The vote split right down the racial divide, with the black members opposing a change and the white members in favor of it. One of the black members summed up the feelings of the others in an interview with Bryant Gumbel, when he said if not for the right to protest, "my grandfather would still be picking somebody's cotton."

On the third reading, the new statute passed when Mayor Young sided with his white brothers and broke the continuing tie. Knowing this was coming, we had been in consultation with Gerald Weber, executive director of the Georgia ACLU, for some weeks. The ACLU quickly filed suit on our behalf, challenging the law as unconstitutional.* Though he granted us a permit to protest, the sheriff decreed that NCWO would be confined to a muddy field three-quarters of a mile away from the gates. The plot, owned and controlled by Augusta National, was below the grade of the street, so even passing cars could not see protesters. The sheriff made it clear in statements to the press that anyone who stepped off the designated area would be arrested. An emergency plea to negate his decision to keep us away from the gates, heard before Judge Dudley Bowen, was denied. We were, literally and figuratively, stuck in the mud.

The club had gone to extraordinary lengths to render our protest ineffective. They were losing the public relations battle, and they reasoned that if the protest could be painted as a failure, they could claim vindication on the question of sex discrimination itself. In an attempt to get a better location, we verbally bargained our request for two hundred people down to one hundred and fifty with the sheriff, but he was unyielding. Though we had been telling the press for weeks that we

---

*NCWO was represented by Bondurant, Mixson & Elmore, one of the top legal firms in Georgia, and Augusta attorney Jack Batson, volunteering for the ACLU. Our case was argued by Sarah Shalf for the firm. Batson's expertise and local knowledge of the Augusta political and social landscape was crucial throughout.

were planning a small gathering, several opposition groups took out permits, with numbers ranging up to five hundred people per group. As a result, members of the press were expecting upwards of one thousand protesters, with some confrontation thrown in.

On the appointed day, our numbers totaled 128 by count—very close to our permitted number. But the opposition mustered fewer than eight people each (the KKK had one). The total effect was that all parties were outnumbered by reporters, photographers, and some two hundred police. Many reporters turned in desperation to the side show aspects of the fringe participants (radio disc jockeys in drag, People Against Ridiculous Protests, an Elvis impersonator) to have something to write about other than a peaceful protest with antidiscrimination speeches. The club's flak, Jim McCarthy, was in the back of the crowd, pushing the number forty as our turnout, and it stuck in some news accounts. Augusta National's statements indicated they viewed the day as a great victory for the right to discriminate against women, attempting to declare the controversy over. We viewed it as a fairly bad scene in a much longer movie.

More than a year (and another Masters Tournament) would pass before the Eleventh Circuit declared the new ordinance unconstitutional. But it had served its purpose—the CEOs were not confronted by protesters as their limousines glided through the front gates of Augusta National Golf Club.

Augusta National Member Profile
William S. (Billy) Morris III,
Morris Communications Corporation, Augusta, Georgia

Morris Communications' small-market family-owned media empire includes some sixty daily, nondaily, and free community newspapers coast to coast; more than thirty radio stations; two radio networks; twenty-five magazines and specialty publications; twenty-seven tourist publications; a book publisher; and online services, outdoor advertising, and printing and marketing operations. The firm began in 1945 when William Morris Jr. bought *The Augusta Chronicle*, founded in 1785.

The Augusta Chronicle kept a steady drumbeat of anti–Martha Burk stories and editorials from the day the controversy became public. In September 2002, William S. Morris III moved a feature on Martha Burk off the front page, killed an accompanying story, and refused to run an article urging the club to open to women for the good of golf and the Masters Tournament (*The Atlanta Journal-Constitution*, 12/13/2002).

The paper always adheres to the club's prohibition on calling the fans a "mob" or anything similar, using the word *patron* instead.

From a former employee:

> Billy Morris is a member of Augusta National as was his father before him. I agree with Martha Burk's correlation between discrimination against women in companies where top management has an affiliation with Augusta National . . . I worked [at Morris] for five years, forced to resign my position at age fifty-five . . . Men were routinely paid more than women because "they had families to support." Interestingly, no one tried to hide it, they just said it right out loud. Funny thing, Morris talks about diversity in the workplace promoting and recruiting minorities. That's about as far as it gets. Just talk.
>
> Top management sets the example, even if it is subliminal. A membership in Augusta communicates that women are second class in the workplace. I've lived it. I believe it.

> [Name withheld], April 6, 2004

Gender Baiting and Bad Girls:
How Women Who Charge Discrimination Are
Punished, Threatened, and Marginalized

Punishing women who speak out dates from antiquity, when women were silenced, threatened, beaten, and sometimes even murdered for defying male cultural norms.[35] Times haven't changed all that much, as I found out when Augusta National hired "PR consultant" Jim McCarthy to manage the crisis they had created for themselves, and to try to stem the tide of negative publicity the club was getting every day. According to Kevin Gover, a lawyer who had dealt with him before, he is "ambitious, unscrupulous . . . attracted to unsavory clients . . . a perfect fit for Augusta."[36] McCarthy's idea was to personalize the conflict (the press was already doing this to a degree anyway) as a face-off between Martha Burk and Hootie Johnson, and demonize me in the process. "The worst thing you can do with an attack activist like Martha Burk is compromise," he said. ". . . you have to go on the attack—investigate the activist . . . take on the press that is often conspiring to give the activists a platform . . ."[37]

As most working women know, the tactics of intimidation

are so familiar I'm surprised there's not a handbook spelling them out. The title could be *How to Defeat Women Who Charge Sex Discrimination.* Chapters would include "Lesbian Baiting," "Discrediting," "Dividing," and "Threats of Violence or Actual Violence." All are standard dirty tricks used to stifle complaints in corporate America. McCarthy had had a good deal of corporate experience, so it was no problem for him to borrow the playbook for Augusta National's benefit.

Whether my personal life was investigated I don't know, since my life situation (married, grandmother of four, unpaid chair of NCWO) did not offer much red meat. But every word I had written publicly was scrutinized, and there was a lot of material, since I had been writing on feminist topics for magazines and newspapers for years. Suddenly the talk-radio jocks and anti-Burk websites seized on a piece I had written for *Ms.* magazine in 1997 titled "The Sperm Stops Here." It was a satire on what would happen if society started to limit men's reproductive choices—a way to put the antiabortion rhetoric in sharp relief. I talked about mandatory contraception for men using something akin to the existing implants for women, and enforcing its use through fertility authorities. As I was forced to repeat dozens of times to the media, anyone who got past fourth grade would recognize that the piece was parody. And in case anyone couldn't see that immediately, the second paragraph began with the words "A modest proposal." But digging it up and trying to convince people it was serious was as good a way as any to paint me as a man-hater.

It's funny how women who are not inclined to accept the status quo are always man-haters and lesbians. Men who challenge the system, meanwhile, are "don't take no for an answer guys" or "aggressive negotiators." A number of anti-Burk

> You and all the other NINJA LES-
> BIANS FROM HELL . . . are a brain
> washing domestic terrorist outfit.
>
> E-mail to NCWO, 2/19/2003

websites came online, one insisting that I was not really a woman. Callers on talk radio frequently asked me if I was married. I always confronted them directly—"What you really want to know is whether I am a lesbian"—usually getting stunned silence in return. Besides, we had already been getting e-mail for months accusing us of being "dykes who hate men," so nothing was new there.

The Lesbian-Baiting Man-Hater idea having fizzled, next came Division. NCWO member groups started getting calls asking if they "agreed with Martha Burk's" campaign on Augusta National. NCWO had by this time taken two votes of affirmation (unanimous) of the campaign just as a statement of solidarity, and I had also been reelected chair for another two-year term (also unanimous). It didn't matter—someone was out to prove our groups were in disagreement, perhaps because dissension in Hootie's own ranks had been reported in *The New York Times*. When no disagreement materialized, a sub-chapter of the General Federation of Women's Clubs, located in Georgia, announced they were resigning from the parent group because they didn't support NCWO. The American Nurses Association (another NCWO member group) got a few calls from disgruntled members, but the "divide and conquer" tactic was also a total washout.

Not only did the club try dividing our member groups, they tried dividing us from women in general and making sure there was publicity. A local group, Women Against Martha Burk (WAMB), was formed, and gave statements to the press about how they didn't agree with us—Augusta National was just fine the way it was. A women's shelter in Augusta sent us a registered letter (printed in *The Augusta Chronicle*) asking for direct funding and accusing us of not caring about everyday women. We

> You don't speak for all women and I hate that you use the word women. It's embarrassing that you are a member of the female species because surely you must have been supposed to be a man. Speaking for all feminine women everywhere.
>
> E-mail to NCWO, 4/2/2003

replied that we engage only in the kind of national advocacy that got the Violence Against Women Act passed so they could get funding in the first place. We suggested that they ask Augusta National Golf Club for local assistance, since the club bragged frequently about its great charitable works. *The Augusta Chronicle* was owned by Billy Morris III, a member of Augusta National. The paper had been extremely hostile to NCWO, but after several conversations with the letters editor, our response to the women was also printed.

Even though the CEOs were staunchly maintaining their silence and their precious memberships, corporate entertainment plans were being canceled or curtailed because the club's attitude made a protest outside the gates inevitable. Many citizens of Augusta rent out their homes for up to $15,000 a week during the Masters Tournament, and local businesses reap a "thirteenth month" of receipts for corporate entertainment that includes liquor, rooms, lavish meals, entertainment, transportation, and gift premiums. Women business owners in Augusta started giving out interviews stating that NCWO wasn't hurting the club with threats of protest, it was hurting female-headed small businesses. The fact that the club was willing to let those small women-owned businesses go without revenue they depended on, just to reinforce the "right" to discriminate against all women, was lost on them.

The golfers had already gotten into the act by trying to divide us from women worldwide. Scott Verplank asked the press rhetorically, "Why don't they do something for the women in Afghanistan?" Talk radio jumped on this one. It gave me a great chance to explain that our groups had in fact been working against the gender apartheid in Afghanistan long before they or George W. Bush had ever heard of the Taliban.

Discrediting was next. Augusta National commissioned a national poll to show that Americans didn't agree with NCWO regarding opening the membership to women. It was what is known in polling parlance as a "push poll," meaning the questions are worded to elicit a certain answer. The actual questions were preceded by a reading of the First Amendment to the Constitution. Then general questions like, "What is the most important issue facing women today?" Much of the poll was aimed directly at Martha Burk, and all characterized the campaign as a personal one—referring to "Martha Burk's demands" quite a number of times.

The results, highly favorable to the club, were announced at a Washington, D.C., news conference orchestrated by McCarthy. NCWO sent Christopher Turman, director of our Women & Social Security Project, because he could blend in with the crowd. The first half

> You are a fucking cunt. I hope you slide under a gas truck and taste your own blood before you die! Another case of some bitch that desperately wants to be a man. Keep the Open ALL MALE unless you want to suck my dick between holes.
>
> E-mail to NCWO, 2/28/2003

hour was devoted to a number of women talking against Martha Burk, including some right-wing think-tankers who were well known in Washington, and a couple of Augustans brought in for the occasion. We really didn't have to do much to turn the tables and discredit the club. National news outlets like the Associated Press, ESPN, and *The Washington Post* consulted legitimate pollsters, who uniformly denounced the poll as so biased and unprofessional that it was meaningless. It was so roundly discredited that ESPN produced a spoof called "Masters Polling Moments," featuring a caricatured Hootie Johnson sitting in front of a fire reading the actual questions.

> This is Russ. I heard your organization was going to castrate one hundred men. Well I'm going to castrate one hundred women. I'm going to cut their pussies out.
>
> Voicemail left on NCWO answering machine, 12/4/2003

Violence, violent rhetoric, or the threat of violence are other ways women are kept in line, and Augusta National used violent imagery without hesitation too. The other things had been annoyances that every women's advocate is accustomed to, but this one got my attention. As the 2003 Masters Tournament neared, NCWO applied for a permit to hold a protest—twelve people on either side of Augusta National's front gates and two hundred across the street. Thanks to the city/county commission's changing the local ordinance on protesting, the sheriff had sole discretion over whether, how long, and in what location a protest could be held. As mentioned in the previous chapter, he designated an open field below the grade of the street, bordered on one side by a large apartment complex with a hundred or so windows looking down on it. Not a comforting thought in a city that was awash in anti-Burk rhetoric, bumper stickers, T-shirts, hats, and buttons, where my face was reportedly stickered on the bottom of urinals all over town, and where gun sales were advertised on local marquees.

Two weeks before the tournament, McCarthy introduced the rhetoric of violence into the discourse. In press interviews, he was using the terms "drive-by shotgunner" and "bomb-thrower" to describe me, but I knew the effect could be to put those ideas into some irate Augusta-defender's head. I was truly alarmed and called Jack Batson, the local ACLU lawyer who was part of the team representing us in the permit matter. Batson and I crafted a "cease and desist" letter over the phone, and I faxed it for delivery to the club, stating truthfully that I believed such rhetoric was irresponsible and put me in danger. Their answer was for McCarthy to repeat his interview to another reporter the next day, this time adding "drive-by shooter" for good measure. A second letter was faxed, reminding the club that they would be held responsible if harm should come to me. It could have been coincidental, but death threats started coming in via e-mail and telephone, with promises to come after us with weapons. I did not go to the press because I didn't want

> When Matthew Sheppard the fag was killed I had a big party with good old fag-hating Americans. When that nigger James Byrd was DRAGGED TO FUCKING DEATH I had a big party with good old nigger hating Americans. I consider you and your little movement DEAD, so I will once again celebrating with good old fag, nigger, communist, socialist hating AMERICANS . . . you fucking piece of garbage.
>
> E-mail to NCWO signed "Ed 'the hatchet' Hitler boom boom out go the lights," 4/12/2003

McCarthy's terminology repeated, which could give more ideas to more nutcases. But I was losing a lot of sleep.

The club never responded to our emergency communications. During the next week, no more McCarthy quotes were printed, though we never knew whether it was because of our letters or because he just couldn't score another interview. I was starting to breathe a little easier—until *Sports Illustrated* came out the week before the protest. It had a chronology of the controversy, and it repeated McCarthy's inflammatory words. A large pull quote from a local citizen in a bar declared, "She oughtta be shot." Furious, I called the editors, accusing them of irresponsible journalism. They offered me a response for the next issue in a regular feature ironically titled "My Shot," which would run a day or so before the tournament. Again not wishing to give any more play to the idea of doing me bodily harm, I declined, but said I would write for the first issue after the tournament. They agreed. "By the way," they added, "we'll pay you $750." "Thanks a whole lot," I replied. "I'll use it to hire a bodyguard."

Nancy Boothe at the Feminist Women's Health Center in Atlanta arranged for the bodyguards, and we rented an SUV with darkly tinted windows to make the trip. Except for the protest itself, I stayed completely out of public view during the forty-eight hours I was in Augusta, Georgia (Jack Batson and spouse Lisa Krisher graciously

> I hope that you die soon and your guts spill out with an unforseen passion all over the Georgia landscape. I WILL BLOW YOUR HEAD OFF WITH MY GLOCK... YOU FUCKING PIECE OF FILTH WHORE. Go die lesbooooooo
>
> E-mail to NCWO with the subject line "Thank God," 4/14/2003

opened their home for me to conduct press interviews and provided a place for our leaders to meet). No harm came to anyone in our group or any of the protesters, but it was no thanks to the Augusta National Golf Club.

The "dirty tricks" used by Augusta National did not originate in the genteel world of golf debate. They're standard fare in corporate America when charges of sex discrimination are raised. I am not suggesting that these tactics are confined to Augusta-related companies or that every single company uses them. But they are routinely used by any firm fighting sex discrimination charges, up to and including threats of violence and rape.[38] Nor are they confined to corporations. The U.S. Air Force Academy, the U.S. Naval Academy, the University of Colorado, and the U.S. Army have all been involved in rape allegation scandals in the past year, where physical violence was used to keep women in line or drum them out of the ranks.

Defending CEO membership in Augusta didn't rise to the level of no-holds-barred, but while Augusta National was busy trashing me in the press and inciting the locals to potential mayhem, women in many of the companies represented in the membership were getting reprimands for speaking up, sometimes accompanied by vague threats to their jobs.

In July 2003, Marie Wilson, president of the Ms. Foundation for Women, arranged a high-level dinner with three male CEOs and other women leaders. The topic was advancing women's leadership, the mission of the nonprofit White House Project that Wilson founded. The idea was to engage male CEOs—the one person in a corporation best positioned to make positive change in advancing women—in an intimate setting to talk about best practices. The dinner was hosted by

Kenneth Chenault, CEO of American Express, and William B. Harrison, CEO of JPMorgan Chase. Both men were members of Augusta National.

When the plans had been announced at a large women's leadership meeting Wilson hosted in Washington, D.C., a couple of months before, I had publicly called on her and JPMorgan Chase CFO Dina Dublon (who was in attendance that day) to challenge the Augusta National memberships when the dinner took place. Both agreed that it needed to be done. Dublon admitted that the Augusta membership had been a topic at JPMorgan Chase for months, with a number of the senior women confronting Harrison. I did not press for an invitation to the dinner myself, but I strongly urged that Jane Smith, CEO of Business and Professional Women/USA, be included. Smith had been outspoken on the Augusta memberships, and as an African American who had experienced both race and sex discrimination, she could challenge these members with authority.

Whether Smith was invited and couldn't make it, or whether the decision was made another way, Dublon was designated as the person who would bring it up. When she did, Wilson asked the men why they didn't simply overrule Hootie Johnson. She correctly pointed out that as CEOs and leaders they would not tolerate a person in their companies doing so much harm, so why would they do it here? And if they couldn't get rid of Johnson, why didn't they merely resign in protest—especially in light of the national controversy that was hurting their corporate images? The questions cast a pall over the room. "It was ridiculous," Wilson would later say. "None of them had any satisfactory answers. They didn't even make any sense. The reasons were nonsensical." The next day, Dublon reportedly was rebuked with a call from John Mack, CEO of Credit Suisse First Boston, and the only man at the dinner not an Augusta member (perhaps he aspires). According to an insider, Mack told her she had been "out of line" to broach the subject of the memberships. It is highly unlikely that the CEO of any company would issue a reprimand to a senior officer from another without the knowledge and approval of her boss. But conveniently for Harrison, he would not be associated with this incident. After that, Dublon told me that the women at her company were no longer interested in talking about Augusta National.

Women in the rank and file at Harrison's company had also questioned his membership at Augusta National for a year, bringing it up repeatedly in meetings, even crafting a letter citing its dampening effect on their ability to work as equals with male colleagues. The letter was quashed when the writer showed it to her bosses and was told it was "hyperpolitical" at the company and could "damage career opportunities." Despite all of this, Harrison doggedly asserted that he was remaining a member.

Dublon's punishment and the letter-quashing were very mild compared to what happens to women who complain about sex discrimination in most companies. The women at Smith Barney (a division of Citigroup, headed by Augusta National member Sanford Weill) brought suit for pervasive sex discrimination in the 1990s. Retaliation was the order of the day. The arrest by police of a plaintiff for "disorderly conduct" outside Carnegie Hall where Weill was presiding over the annual meeting looked mild by comparison. In litigation against Bank of America (headed by Augusta member Kenneth Lewis) and Morgan Stanley (you guessed it—Augusta member Philip Purcell) as well as a host of other companies headed by the green jackets, women have been subjected to the following tactics and worse:

A female trader at Citigroup was given a golf putter made of a bull's penis on a company outing.[39]

Women at Smith Barney were routinely left out of golf outings with their peers and bosses, called "cunts" and "whores," and sent penis-shaped baked goods. Men who were not interested in the degrading sexual tricks were sometimes chided as wimps or told that they were not team players. When the women complained, they were physically threatened, fired, and later subjected to hours of grilling about their personal lives in depositions set up by the company.[40]

Morgan Stanley managers not only excluded women executives from golf outings with clients, they entertained clients at strip clubs. When they fired the complainant and the government sued on her behalf, they tried to blame her dismissal on her own behavior.[41]

Bank of America was sued by a former analyst who described an extremely vulgar work environment in January 2003, as the Augusta National controversy reached a crescendo. By May, just after CEO Kenneth Lewis joined both his CFO and former bank chairman Hootie Johnson as an Augusta National member, the bank sponsored Annika Sorenstam as the first woman to compete in a PGA Tour event in fifty-eight years. Bank of America was looking like a great friend of women.[42]

The incidents above began before the world knew about secret memberships in the green jacket cult, and they give lie to the claim that a CEO's "personal membership" in a discriminatory club is no indication of how his company will behave toward its female employees. All of these men had the power to order straightforward investigations of the sex discrimination in their firms, punish the perpetrators instead of letting them off the hook through transfers and retirements, and direct the companies they headed to clean up their acts. But they didn't do that, even in the service of the precious bottom line. Estimates are that the ultimate settlements in these cases alone will cost hundreds of millions of dollars.

There is no question that retaliation in a variety of forms is visited on women who complain in many, many companies—not just those headed by men who happen to do business at clubs that keep women out. But it's all part of a pattern of corporate misogyny that belies the fancy statements about equality and diversity. In the Augusta controversy, punishment even spilled over to a charity benefitting women. Stephanie Davis, CEO of the Atlanta Women's Foundation, had been an outspoken critic of the club's policies from the beginning. She was an invaluable resource in helping NCWO navigate the local political landscape and in pulling together a meeting hosted by Atlanta Mayor Shirley Franklin for opinion leaders to discuss the situation. When the foundation announced the speaker—Martha Burk—for the spring fund-raising event, a long-term corporate supporter immediately withdrew its annual $50,000 contribution.[43] The CEO was not a member of Augusta National, but apparently didn't want to antagonize his buddies who were.

Given "business as usual" in corporate America when

it comes to sex discrimination, it's not surprising that the members of Augusta National, the most powerful businessmen in the nation, did not discourage the club's tactics. They knew McCarthy had been hired (some members were even present at his interview).[44] They knew the club had commissioned a "poll" to discredit me and take attention away from the issue of sex discrimination. They knew "talking points" had been distributed to the media, and that the local law enforcement establishment had been used to change the law and intimidate us. They knew the women in their companies, the stockholders, and many of the customers were unhappy with what they were doing. The fact that they chose to remain silent was a loud statement about a "woman's place" indeed.

Augusta National Member Profile
Sanford I. Weill, chair and former CEO, Citigroup

Sanford I. Weill was the highest-paid corporate executive in the United States in 2003, pulling down $63 million. He started on Wall Street as a $35-a-week clerk, and eventually founded his own brokerage firm. In 1986 he bought Commercial Credit, a loan company described by his assistant, Alison Falls, as a "loan-sharking" operation. Through a series of mergers and acquisitions, including Salomon Smith Barney, the firm eventually morphed into Citigroup.

Weill presided over the company during the infamous "Boom Boom Room" years at Smith Barney, when women were repeatedly sexually harassed and male brokers hung a toilet from the ceiling and mixed drinks in a garbage can in the basement of the Garden City brokerage office. The company engaged in particularly brutal tactics during litigation, using what is known as the "nuts-or-sluts" defense: In harassment or discrimination cases, paint the woman as promiscuous, crazy, or unstable. One plaintiff was singled out by police for arrest outside a stockholders' meeting where Weill was presiding.

Two of Weill's board members, George David and Kenneth Derr, are members of Augusta National, as is former CEO John Reed. Weill serves on the Committee to Encourage Corporate Philanthropy with fellow club members Kenneth Chenault, Kenneth Lewis, Warren Buffett, Philip Purcell, and Arthur Ryan. He serves on the board of Memorial Sloan-Kettering Cancer Center with William B. Harrison, and he is a former director of AT&T, headed by David Dorman.

In the summer of 2003, I ran into Weill at a restaurant in New York. We had a cordial conversation, and he agreed to meet with me, asking that my office call in September for a meeting date. We called at least ten times and were never given a date. After I mentioned Weill's membership to Robert Rubin, a close Weill advisor, some months later, Citigroup suddenly called back (it could have been coincidental). The meeting would be with several senior company representatives, led by senior vice president Michael Schlein, but would not include Weill. I reluctantly agreed, but stated that I expected Weill to make good on his word at a later time. He never did, though I repeated my request in writing after the meeting with his staff took place.

The Citigroup representatives excused Weill's membership as "personal," having nothing to do with the company. When asked if they would put forth the same argument if he was a member of a club that discriminated on the basis of race, I was greeted with stone-cold silence.

Press reports indicate that the company spends several hundred thousand dollars per year on entertainment at Augusta, which includes hotel rooms, parties in rented lavish private homes, catered meals, open bars, and amusement. Weill presides over the festivities.

Mixed Messages in the Marketplace

Women Have Conquered the Workplace—
I Read It in *BusinessWeek*

"If we talk the talk, we don't have to walk the walk on women's progress," could be the official motto of twenty-first-century corporate America. In the 1960s and 1970s, employment laws outlawing outright discrimination were passed and affirmative-action-plan requirements for companies doing business with the government were established. Since then it's been one long game of dodge the issue, hide-the-discrimination behind programs, hire public relations people to spin poor progress, and generally "outsource the woman (and minority men) problem" without actually having to do much about it. So far the laws have hardly worked at all, but the dodge-the-issue game has worked pretty well.

Let's take one small example to illustrate how this game is played, though it's replicated countless times in countless companies year after year. Think of it as the *BusinessWeek* tactic, after an article that appeared in that magazine on July 28, 2003, entitled "Crashing GE's Glass Ceiling." The timing of the article was no accident. The Augusta National membership list had now been public for nine months, and GE's CEO, Jeffrey Immelt, was on it. He had refused to resign the membership, even though the very fact of it was contrary to company statements about fairness and diversity. In national media appearances, NCWO had repeatedly singled him out, along with other prominent CEOs, as examples of corporate hypocrisy. Our comments were simple and to the point: Regardless of company rhetoric, CEO membership in a club where high-level business is done and where women are kept out makes a clear statement about how they, and by extension their companies, really value women. We always added another simple truth—if the issue were race they would not maintain the memberships nor the stone wall of solidarity in refusing to resign or even to speak out against the discriminatory policies.

GE's public relations folks must have gone into overdrive, because the piece they succeeded in placing with *BusinessWeek* was replete with the same hypocrisy surrounding Immelt's Augusta National membership, and clearly designed to defuse the negative publicity he had attracted. The article was a fine example of the media collusion that contributes to a skewed perception in the national dialogue about how far women have come, and the author used several tactics that are now stock-in-trade for companies in talking about women in corporate America.

Promulgate the myth that women are doing great and have no barriers. "Crashing GE's Glass Ceiling" said it all. The focus was Charlene Begley, the first woman at GE to head a major unit "among a generation of executives who may find room at the top." The article identified Begley as a "mother of three" even before giving her new title—showing, of course, that women can indeed have it all in an enlightened company. Trashing the old GE under former CEO Jack Welch in the first paragraph as a "bastion of back-slapping overachievers . . . who were expected to move to places like Erie, Pennsylvania, on a moment's notice to advance their careers," the paragraph touted the fact that Begley doesn't work weekends. Slipped in a page later is the information that she has worked in twenty locations (including Erie) over a fifteen year period, and far down in the piece we learn that her husband is a stay-at-home dad because GE's policies are still constructed for workers who can "move around the world on short assignments."

Build up your management as dedicated to change. "[Former CEO] Jack Welch, who had a mediocre record on diversity and used to sneer openly at the idea of 'work-life balance,' has retired. In his place is Jeffrey R. Immelt, 47, who came of age in an era of feminism . . ." The article continued, reporting that Immelt had just *appointed a woman* as chief marketing officer. Readers were apparently expected to be dazzled by this and ignore the numbers in the next paragraph. Presented positively as evidence of improvement, they not only showed that GE still had a lousy record for women in management under Immelt's leadership, but the company was even below the extremely poor average for the Fortune 500. So much for that feminist upbringing.

Get women to discount sex discrimination as a workplace factor. "Begley fought to get into the financial management program at GE . . . She won the job . . . Begley, who says she never encountered any sexism in the company en route to the top, is classic GE, impatient, smart, and driven to succeed. She even plays golf . . . [in a former position at GE] she nixed the practice of mandatory meetings to discuss diversity efforts, saying it felt forced . . . 'I want no part of being treated differently because I'm a woman.'" When another woman, who started the GE Women's Network, is quoted as saying the company's practices presented clear barriers to women trying to reach the executive ranks, Begley undermines her view by saying she initially participated in the network grudgingly because she didn't think it was necessary. Even while giving lip service to the mentoring the network affords, Begley all but damns it as a kaffeeklatsch where women talk to one another to feel better.

In Begley, we find a woman who is performing a truly valuable service for the company. She is denying the evidence of pay and promotion discrimination that the numbers at GE clearly demonstrate, she is accepting a work-life model normed on men with stay-at-home wives as appropriate to today's workplace, and she is stating that any woman who can't make it in that environment just isn't trying hard enough. No wonder she keeps getting promoted.

Create lots of programs and slick brochures, claiming to be changing the system. "Immelt, who asked Catalyst [an organization that tracks women in business] to advise the company three years ago and joined its board in 2001, says Begley is just the most prominent of numerous female executives who are rising fast at GE." The article does not mention that because Immelt is a board member of Catalyst, GE gives the organization an annual donation (widely believed to be between $25,000 and $50,000 a year). In turn GE gets the Catalyst annual "award" for "programs" like the GE Women's Network, which don't necessarily work but look good on paper.

So here we have a high-profile article in a major business publication telling us that companies are family friendly, women are making great strides (those who aren't are personally lacking), and we're just around the corner from complete parity with men. Articles are one thing, and there is no question that enough of them appearing in enough places have the power to change perception about what is going on in the workplace for women.[45] But a well-developed system to perpetuate the equality-in-the-workplace myth can go much further, if it is used correctly. And that brings us to the final tactic.

Spin your poor numbers into gold. "We've got an excellent pipeline," Immelt gushes. His words do not match reality, even as it is presented in the best possible light in the article. Doing the math on the numbers scattered in the text, we find that while 16,000 women belong to the GE Women's Network (and not all GE women are members), the company has only 22 female officers out of the 173 total. So far fewer than 1 percent of the women in the network have made it to officer level. Hardly a brimming pipeline, and hardly an effective vehicle for advancing women. One more thing: Since Immelt became CEO, three new board members have been appointed—all white men. It would be interesting to know whether any of them were recruited on the links at Augusta National Golf Club.

Women Are Rushing Home—
I Read It in *The New York Times*

In October 2003, *The New York Times Magazine* ran a cover story by Lisa Belkin: "The Opt-Out Revolution." On the cover were the words "Q: Why Don't More Women Get to the Top? A: They Choose Not To. Abandoning the Climb and Heading Home." The premise of the story, neatly embodied in its title, was this: While women aren't getting ahead in the workplace as fast as everyone hoped a generation ago when females flooded the labor market on the crest of the women's movement and in the wake of new laws against employment discrimination, it's not because of lingering sex discrimination. To the contrary, women are seeing the light—the workplace is not for them. Women don't choose to succeed.

The line above the title, "Many high-powered women today don't ever hit the glass ceiling, choosing to leave the workplace for motherhood. Is this the failure of one movement or the beginning of another?" Never mind that a careful reading revealed that of the eight Princeton-educated upper-class white women Belkin interviewed, all but one had left the workplace for reasons other than pure choice. After a catalog of workplace ills beginning with the huge problems faced by working mothers with unresponsive bosses and rigid institutions, and ending with the statement that "being successful required becoming a man," Belkin concluded that women don't run the world because "maybe they don't want to," even implying at one point that mothers have genes that make them want to drop out. Without acknowledging that her data strongly indicate that the structure of the workplace is itself a form of systemic sex discrimination, the article belatedly admitted that quitting is driven as much by job dissatisfaction as by the pull of motherhood.

Belkin's piece caused a firestorm of counterpunches and protests from working women and those who had left the marketplace involuntarily or out of frustration. This was not surprising, given that half of the workforce is female, and 79 percent of women who maintain families are working.[46] And never mind the fact that unlike Belkin's Princeton group (all married to successful men whose jobs could sustain a family alone), most women go to work for the same reasons men do: They need to support their families, and work is rewarding psychologically.

What was surprising was that Belkin's article caused such an outcry, when in fact it was part of a drumbeat of conservative rhetoric about women and work that started a generation ago, roughly coinciding with the election of Ronald Reagan. The move to "turn the clock back to 1954"[47] with dismantling of women's rights as its centerpiece was expertly chronicled in 1991 by Susan Faludi in *Backlash: The Undeclared War Against American Women*. *Backlash* detailed a cultural war that played out in the media:

> In the last decade, publications from *The New York Times* to *Vanity Fair* to *The Nation* have issued a steady stream of indictments against the women's movement, with such headlines as WHEN FEMINISM FAILED OR THE AWFUL TRUTH ABOUT WOMEN'S LIB. They hold the campaign for women's equality responsible for nearly every woe besetting women, from mental depression to meager savings accounts . . . in Hollywood films, of which *Fatal Attraction* is only the most famous, emancipated women with condominiums of

their own slink wild-eyed between bare walls, paying for
their liberty with an empty bed, a barren womb . . . In
prime-time television shows, from "thirtysomething" to
"Family Man," single, professional, and feminist women
are humiliated, turned into harpies, or hit by nervous
breakdowns; the wise ones recant their independent ways
by the closing sequence.[48]

This cultural revolution was backed by the New Right agenda
that embodied legislation ranging from outright abortion bans
to revocation of the Equal Pay Act and other equal employment laws.[49]

Antifeminism was at the center of a right-wing agenda successfully infused into politics and culture by such individuals as
Jerry Falwell, and institutions like the Heritage Foundation and
American Enterprise Institute (AEI). It picked up steam in the
1990s with the founding of some conservative women's groups
like the Independent Women's Forum (IWF) and the Clare
Booth Luce Policy Institute. Bankrolled with the same right-
wing money that turned Heritage and AEI into policy power-
houses in the 1980s, these groups exist solely to sell the idea
that any shortcomings women experience, like unequal pay or
glass ceilings, are in fact due only to women's choices. Any
other explanation is a product of feminist imagination.

Six years after Faludi called attention to the media backlash, the IWF published *Women's Figures,* a carefully spun
reinterpretation of wage and salary data purporting to show
that the pay gap between women and men is due not to gender discrimination but to that unfilled pipeline, and to women
"choosing" work that is devalued compared to jobs men
choose. Conservative author George Will[50] and news outlets

like *The Wall Street Journal* pounced on the report as evidence that women really do prefer the lower-wage work and don't mind the lack of workplace supports that force many to head home for lack of child care or humane hours.[51] Even Marilyn vos Savant, the *Parade* magazine guru touted as one of the most intelligent people on earth, joined the party. She published her own Q&A column about sex roles in society—presenting the worst stereotypes as truths most people hold dear (men are better surgeons, women are less dedicated and more dispensable workers).[52]

Belkin's "back to home and hearth" pseudomovement was no temporary reprise of a media flurry that peaked in the 1980s. The backlash that Faludi had documented continued to build throughout the 1990s, showing no signs of abating as the new century began. Main myth number two, that boys are now the oppressed minority in schools, was first pushed to the forefront in 1999 with Christina Hoff Sommers's book *The War Against Boys: How Misguided Feminism Is Harming Our Young Men.* By May 2003, it was given mainstream credibility in a *BusinessWeek* cover story entitled "The New Gender Gap," featuring a smirking girl towering over a worried boy with a subtitle "Why boys are falling behind girls in education—and what it means for the economy, business, and society." The piece, amply illustrated with downcast boys and self-satisfied girls, used such phrases as "gender takeover," "anti-boy culture," "education grab by girls," and said the reverse gender gap was projected to "get worse." It further opined that the underachievement of boys could be due to "downsized dads cast adrift in the New Economy," and it ended with an all-too-familiar conclusion: "A new world has opened up for girls, but unless a symmetrical effort is made to help boys find their footing, it may turn out that it's a lonely place to be."[53]

While statistics on school enrollments and achievement levels showing progress in selected areas for girls were presumably accurate, they obscured a larger picture and presented school achievement as a zero-sum game, with the boys losing. Educational gender equity experts like David Sadker were drowned out when they countered with the statistics showing that college programs, while now populated by more females than males, are still highly segregated (women earn between 75 percent and 90 percent of degrees in education, nursing, home economics, library science, social work, and psychology), and that computer science and technology reflect increasing male-dominated gender disparities.[54]

> It's not just women who are disappointed that modern life has not accommodated their various needs. So are millions of baby-boomer men who wanted their marriage to be a genuine partnership of equals . . . so long as [wives] stay out of the labor market, husbands are trapped in it . . . Hence that familiar social phenomenon: a married couple in their 50s in which the wife is resentful because she does too little paid work and the husband is resentful because he does too much.
>
> Michael Elliott, "Men Want Change Too," *Time*, 3/22/2004, p. 59

In the midst of worsening news on the war in Iraq and only a week after terrorist bombings in Madrid killed hundreds, *Time* gave its March 22, 2004, cover to another "opting out" story, "The Case for Staying Home: Why More Young Moms Are Opting Out of the Rat Race." The photo was of a plaintive little boy clinging to his mother hopefully. In an article somewhat more balanced than the Belkin piece, author Claudia Wallis pointed to the lack of decent child care options and unrealistically long hours as the driving forces behind workplace defections on the part of higher-income women. Sociologist Pamela Stone summed it up: "Despite all the family-friendly rhetoric, the workplace for professionals is extremely, extremely inflexible." A sidebar acknowledged that most women do not have the luxury of quitting ("it is no longer possible to support a middle-class family on Dad's income alone"), and another sidebar by Michael Elliot made the case for more humane workplaces for men too. Nods to reality notwithstanding, the overall effect was a strong impression that the mass exodus of women from paid work continues unabated.[55]

The net effect of these two negative contemporary myths is a very mixed message that goes something like this: "Girls are getting all the opportunities now, to the detriment of boys. Soon the educated workforce will be female-dominated and command all the good jobs, displacing the rightful owners. But women can't handle the good jobs—they're not geared for the demands. They really want to stay home and nurture the kids while Dad brings home the bacon."

Women Will Get There— We Just Have to Hone Our Skills

Not all of the current "advice" and "analysis" of women's place in the world of work is of the backlash variety cited above, but it can be just as harmful. In non-backlash popular business literature, the slow pace of women in achieving power in comparable numbers to men is most often blamed on women's inability or unwillingness to adapt to workplace standards. Never mind that those standards were constructed around one-earner families of generations past when most women stayed home (a reality acknowledged even by some of the backlashers). Failure to change that model has resulted in a generation's worth of self-improvement books for women who must not only fit into a mold cast for men—in some cases we have virtual handbooks on how to become junior men.

The modern genre started in the 1970s with *Dress for Success* by John Malloy, a book that told women how to dress professionally (like a man) at work. It was good advice, because men didn't take females all that seriously anyway— most were in support jobs like secretary—and people like to promote others who look like them. Since then, there has been a steady stream of advice: *Going to the Top: A Road Map for Success from America's Leading Women Executives; Be Your Own Mentor; What's Holding You Back?; Hardball for Women; Play Like a Man, Win Like a Woman; Why Good Girls Don't Get Ahead . . . But Gutsy Girls Do;* and last year's best-seller *Nice Girls Don't Get the Corner Office: 101 Unconscious Mistakes Women Make That Sabotage Their Careers.*

Much of the advice given in these books is very good. Everyone has to have a certain level of competence to get ahead, and everyone has to operate in the environment in which they find themselves. When business self-help books first gained popularity, women were new to the game of corporate advancement, and it was unquestionably a man's world. But what's so discouraging about it is that thirty years after Malloy started it all, it's still necessary to advise women as if the workplace really belongs to men—*because it still does.* Back then we didn't know how rigged the game was;

now we just accept it. With a self-improvement industry that has been going strong for a generation now, it's no wonder women have been conditioned to think they have to have one more degree, one more seminar, so many more years of experience, or one more rotation through the feeder jobs before moving up. Men, with their entirely different conditioning and attitudes, just take the promotion and figure out how to do the actual job later.

Very few advice volumes have attacked the business environment itself—that's left to policy wonks and think-tankers whose work never reaches the popular marketplace. The books tell us that women just need to hone their skills, interaction styles, attitudes—and, oh yeah, wait till that pipeline gets full (never mind that it's been a generation, and we're still waiting). The responsibility is always on the individual woman. Nobody every puts any responsibility on those in power—and unless we do, our daughters and granddaughters will be reading these same books, only with different titles.

The problem with the mold self-improvement books are cast in is that they will get some individual women to the top, but they are not systemic solutions to systemic problems. One thing all have right—at least so far—is that with very few exceptions, women still have to play by the men's rules on the men's playground. But it's changing the playground that's so important. Former U.S. Representative Patricia Schroeder (D-CO), who was the leader of the women's caucus in Congress during the 1970s and 1980s, used to talk about the notion of a *critical mass* before permanent change can come about. It doesn't have to be half (Schroeder thought 100 women in the 435-member House would be enough), but it has to be a high enough number that people can't be pigeonholed, thought of as an exception to the norm, or deemed a "special interest" group. Gail Evans, CNN's first female vice president, captured the concept of critical mass in *She Wins, You Win*. Evans understood that systemic change can only come about when women aren't "special cases." When there is a "women's team" and women are dedicated to increasing their numbers at every level up the power ladder, systemic change is possible.

Cleary, it's time for a reality check.

That old adage about not believing everything you read is good advice. The pay gap—even according to the conservative Bush administration—is real. The time crunch is real too, and so is the fact that most women are working, will continue to work, and need the money.

The women's movement is often blamed for turning women into unhappy wage slaves by opening up the job possibilities through a combination of legislation and education. But that simplistic notion masks a larger truth. At the same time that "women's liberation" (as it was dubbed at the time) of the 1970s was gaining traction, the economy was beginning a fundamental shift. As real earnings declined, it became harder and harder for a single-earner family to sustain a middle-class lifestyle. In the years following World War II, U.S. workers had enjoyed strong wage growth that outpaced inflation and lifted living standards. But after 1972, when real average weekly wages hit their postwar peak, U.S. workers began to experience a steady decline in living standards as wage growth lagged behind the sky-rocketing costs of living.[56] While working-class women's jobs had been crucial to their families' financial well-being for years, Ward Cleaver now needed June to get a job. The women's movement just made it possible for her to work at something other than teaching or nursing.

Nowhere in the "opt-out" or "girls are taking over" stories do we find acknowledgment that women are entitled to seek fulfillment through education and work. Nor do we find acknowledgment that 49 percent of adult women in this country are single[57] and the fairy godmother is not sending a monthly check. Quite the opposite: We're almost back to that 1954 idea that it's only "okay" for women to work if it doesn't interfere with the family. Called the "new momism" by authors Susan Douglas and Meredith Michaels in their 2004 book *The Mommy Myth,* the culture is now reasserting that "to be a remotely decent mother, a woman has to devote her entire physical, psychological, emotional, and intellectual being, 24/7, to her children." Unfortunately, too many of us, women and men alike, are still playing old tapes in our heads, left over from decades of sex-role stereotyping in the culture: *The jobs really belong to men first; men are entitled to fulfilling work outside the home and women must prove necessity; men are generally better at the jobs, though an occasional woman can be an exception to the rule.*

When it comes to job ownership, thinking in the culture must change. Most opposition to affirmative action and even corporate programs designed to advance women are based on the notion that women are "taking" something from the rightful owners. If the pool of jobs could be viewed as belonging to everyone, not just one group, then it's clear that the men who have controlled the top for centuries have more than their share, and the women who have provided the support systems have more than their share down at the lower levels. (Men also have less than their share of time they could spend with their families.) If we further adjust our thinking about men's competence always being higher, it would automatically broaden the pool of candidates for any job, taking women out of the "special case" category. Considering women needs to become "normal" and automatic. That's where the critical mass comes in. Remember, with a critical mass, when one of your own is proposed, it's harder for others to charge that the nomination is because a small minority is "pushing an agenda." Of course, females wouldn't get hired every time, but at least the genders would have a truly equal chance to compete.

Even if work were not a necessity for most women, we don't openly question the basic assumption that it's fine for men to have enrichment through fulfilling jobs outside the home, but it's not okay for women. Do women "have" to work in order to make it acceptable? Corporate America is still mostly operating on the stay-at-home mom/organization-man dad model, and almost everyone is the worse off for it. Men ought to be entitled to policies that don't make them automatons and slaves to the workplace either. The corporate elites don't feel this (all that "working" golf and "client entertainment"), and men have a better shot than women at getting to be a member of that elite, so they emulate the higher-ups and perpetuate the model.

Bothersome though they might be, it's time to look at the facts.[58, 59, 60, 61, 62, 63]

Though the overall gap in pay between women and men working full-time year-round in 2004 was 23 percent, an analysis of women and men who had earnings in each of the last fifteen years revealed that women made only 57 cents on the dollar, or a pay gap of 43 percent.

Women in their *prime earning years* make only 38 percent of what men earn, due to fewer work hours and the care-giving responsibilities not imposed on men.

Equal pay is a problem in every occupational category, with professional and technical women earning 27 percent less than males, office and administrative support 12 percent less, sales 38 percent less, service 16 percent less, medicine 41 percent less, college faculty 21 percent less, lawyers 13 percent less, and computer scientists and systems analysts 19 percent less.

Women are only 5.2 percent of top earners in the Fortune 500.

Women are the majority of professional employees.

Close to 90 percent of board seats in the largest 1,000 corporations are held by men.

98 percent of CEOs in the Fortune 500 are male.

Labor force participation has increased most dramatically among married women. 63 percent of women work more than forty hours per week, and 68 percent of married working mothers put in forty or more hours per week.

42 percent of female executives have no children; 1 percent of male executives are childless.

Since 1977 the number of hours worked by dual- and single-earner couples has increased twelve hours per week. Americans work longer hours than those in other developed countries.

Women have been earning more bachelor's and master's degrees than men since the 1980s.

Women's enrollment in business schools has been declining since the mid-1990s.

24,362 sexual harassment cases were filed with the EEOC in 2003.

If we really want to get some insight into contemporary workplace reality, some of these statistics bear further scrutiny. The fact that women are now the majority of professional employees looks pretty good, doesn't it? Yep. On the surface. But look closer at the category "professional employees" and you find that social workers, registered nurses, elementary and middle school teachers, and psychologists are included, and more than 90 percent of these workers are female. Engineering, on the other hand, is still 89 percent male.[64] A more realistic look at *corporate* America comes from the statistics on boards and CEOs and reports like the one on Wal-Mart, where women hold 70 percent of the jobs overall but only 14.3 percent of management positions. And that statistic about women in business schools is disturbing indeed.

But Discrimination in Employment Is Against the Law

The 1963 Equal Pay Act (EPA) and Title VII of the 1964 Civil Rights Act are our oldest and strongest federal statutes against sex discrimination. The Equal Pay Act was intended to end blatant discrimination—before its passage, it was legal to restrict jobs to "men only" and to pay women less for doing the same work as men. Sound familiar? The Civil Rights Act made sex discrimination at work (including sexual harassment, courts would later rule) illegal, albeit as an unintended consequence of ending race discrimination in employment. Those "Help Wanted: Male" (with their implied *white* as a qualifier) ads disappeared. Women and minority men began, ever so slowly, to be considered for jobs formerly reserved for white men. Some would say it was the first crack in the glass ceiling, though the term hadn't been invented yet. But if it was a crack, it was only a hairline, and it hasn't widened much since. Women are still 92 percent of nurses, 97 percent of receptionists, 98 percent of preschool teachers, and 64 percent of store clerks—all jobs found in the "Help Wanted: Female" sections of those 1964 classifieds.

When President Kennedy signed the Equal Pay Act, the pay gap between men and women working full-time year-round was 40 percent.[65] Women everywhere assumed that the legal protection would mean a rapid shrinking of the difference. And it did shrink, but not nearly fast enough. Forty-one years (and a whole working life) later, women had gained a measly 17 cents, and some of *that* was from erosion of men's wages, not increases in female pay. That means a whole generation of working women somehow missed out on the revolution that the Equal Pay Act promised. Women of color are still furthest behind: African-American females earned 64 cents to the 2004 white man's dollar, and Hispanic women only 52 cents. Over a career, the pay gap costs the average woman around a half million dollars—the difference between your kids going to college and flipping burgers, the difference between owning a home and renting, the difference between a secure retirement and living your old age on the edge or in genteel poverty.

The pay gap is not restricted to the higher echelons. Male teachers and nurses make more than women in those jobs, and clerks at Wal-Mart are better paid if they happen to be male. But the higher you go, the wider the gap.[66]

What went wrong? Like Augusta National's claim that it is "happily entwined" with the Masters Golf Tournament it owns and controls, the pay gap and the promotion gap are "unhappily twisted" into a rope that strangles workplace progress. Experts most often cite three strands of the rope: continuing job segregation, narrow court rulings, and enforcement gaps.

Supporters of equal pay legislation recognized job segregation as a problem from the day the first Equal Pay Act was introduced in 1945 until a bill passed eighteen years later. Despite the thousands of "Rosie the Riveters" who had performed so-called "men's jobs" during World War II, post-war women were banished back home or to the female job ghetto when the war ended. The prevailing cultural ideal at the time was a family unit with a wage-earning father and stay-at-home mother who might decide to work for "extras," but whose earnings were not really needed.

The majority of working women, particularly those in the union movement who held jobs in factories, knew better. They knew their families needed their paychecks to live, and they knew that the mere designation of some jobs as "women's jobs" caused employers to devalue their worth. Despite a long battle for equal pay legislation to include equal pay for work of "comparable character" (which would have forced employers to look beyond the sex of the worker performing a job, and evaluate the worth of the work itself), final language was limited to prohibiting wage discrimination "for equal work."

Efforts to broaden the concept of equal pay beyond women and men doing virtually the same job had failed. Employers had no need to compare job duties when setting wage rates— so packing jobs (women) in tobacco plants and canneries would continue to be valued lower and paid less by employers than floor sweeping jobs (men) in the same facilities.[67]

Courts have generally interpreted the Equal Pay Act as applying to jobs that are exactly the same, or nearly the same, and allowing, as the law requires, for differences in seniority, merit, or productivity if the job involves "piece work." So if you're on an assembly line and you have the same experience and tenure as the guy next to you, the courts will come down on your side if the employer pays you less and you sue. And if you are a department head with essentially the same duties, responsibilities, and skills as a male department head who is paid more, you most likely will prevail, even if the departments you oversee have different functions. But if you perform a job with a "core of tasks" that is the same as some other male-held jobs but there are even small differences in other tasks or requirements, you will probably lose under the Equal Pay Act.[68]

Even though all jobs (except some in the military) are technically now open to both genders, we still have a good deal of job segregation, and so-called "women's jobs" are still undervalued compared to "men's jobs." There is still no federal law requiring job comparisons in setting wages and salaries. Some of the modern equivalents to the packing plant examples above—where the predominantly female jobs are undervalued and underpaid compared to the predominantly male jobs—are social workers versus parole officers, school food servers versus school janitors, clerical supervisors versus dock foremen, animal wardens ("dog pound" workers) versus child care workers, and vice president for Human Resources versus vice president for Finance.

Lack of enforcement is another problem, both for EPA and Title VII violations. The Equal Employment Opportunity Commission (EEOC), part of the U.S. Department of Labor, is charged with monitoring compliance and screening complaints. During the Reagan and Bush I presidencies, enforcement personnel and funding were cut drastically. Though the Clinton administration stepped up enforcement in comparison, the agency never recovered from the 1980–1992 cuts.

But the experts, right as they are to look at limits in the law, job segregation, and enforcement gaps, have missed more fundamental reasons why the pay gap is so stubborn and the glass ceiling is still firmly in place (one wag said it's because it's being weighted down by a very thick layer of men). Go back to the idea of those *systemic barriers,* like the ones women faced in getting credit before 1974. While a few individual women "make it" past these built-in barriers and join the men at the top, women *as a group* cannot overcome bias that is built into the system by *individually* using the legal structure we have now. Class actions—where groups of women band together to bring a lawsuit—are slightly more effective, but they are extremely hard to put together. It can take years just to get class certification (the right to bring a group action), much less a monetary award, from the courts.

So forty-plus years after most laws protecting women were passed, we are still fighting, seemingly piece by piece, to make those laws work. Why? To put it simply, our laws were crafted using a faulty paradigm—they were cast in a mold destined to fail. Consider the Equal Pay Act. We've already seen that protections are minimal, basically confined to equal pay for *exactly* the same job. Even if that is your situation and you know it, it's no easy task to get satisfaction under the EPA. That's because the EPA—like Title VII (which affords you a little more protection at least in hiring, sexual harassment, and promotion), Equal Credit, Title IX, and laws prohibiting employers from firing you because you're pregnant—is *complaint driven*. The paradigm is this: Employers are not *required* to do anything positive vis-à-vis women's employment. It's true that by law they can't have explicit policies that say "no women allowed" or "we pay men more." But beyond that, they're not required to hire you, evaluate your job or your pay relative to men, promote you, or retain you instead of the guy next to you when hard times hit.

Under the complaint-driven model, employers are merely *prohibited from discriminating* on the basis of sex. And there is no one looking over their shoulders to monitor compliance with that prohibition. All a company has to do is sit back and wait until they're sued to even look at pay and promotion data or internal practices. (Even the much-vaunted affirmative action, often characterized as a quota system for women and minority men, applies only to companies holding federal contracts. They must promise not to discriminate and they must have written "goals and timetables." Nothing more.)

In practical terms, the complaint-driven paradigm means the burden of ensuring compliance is entirely on the woman. To get an employer to change a discriminatory practice, you must at some level initiate and follow through on a complaint. This can range from a word with your supervisor to a full-fledged lawsuit. Readers will already have recognized the pitfalls of this approach. Even a small mention of possible unfairness can cause you to be labeled a "whiner." If it gets to the formal complaint stage, you're a "troublemaker." At that point retaliation can set in, which can take many forms. You may be fired (for unrelated reasons, of course), frozen out of office interactions, given less desirable assignments, given a tougher work schedule. File a lawsuit, and it's all-out war. The fact that retaliation is against the law once a complaint has been filed has little weight here. The practical effect is that in addition to proving the discrimination, a woman must also prove the retaliation. It's no wonder that most women, at some point in this process, just move on to another job. As the woman at *Golf Digest* reminded us, even that solution can be hard if word gets around an industry that an individual has complained.

> Mr. McAnally responded to the women's complaints by distributing around the office copies of a magazine article titled "Stop Whining" that warned, "constant complaining can cost you your job."
>
> "Panel Finds Bias Against Women at Merrill Lynch," *The New York Times,* 4/21/2004

Women who do stay and fight must be prepared for a long haul, usually years of discovery, depositions, hearings, and postponements before they see a day in court. Obviously this can cost thousands, or even hundreds of thousands of dollars. And women can be subjected to an unbelievable array of adverse outcomes at the hands of the company. High-profile cases from the recent past have shown that lawyers can legally ask about your sex life, subpoena your medical records, force psychological examinations, and talk to anyone they want to about you, including abusive ex-spouses.[69]

Now let's look at the complaint-driven paradigm again, taking these very real outcomes into account. All the marbles are on one side: the company's. It has strong resources—money, on-staff attorneys, and a corporate culture that not only discourages or prevents complaints[70] but also enforces sanctions on those who dare raise their voices. The company has all the time in the world to fight. In fact, it's in their best interests to drag things out and create as many obstacles as possible. That way the woman will likely give up or run out of money. Few women can afford to hire lawyers and go against the clout of mega-corporations, drag through the courts for years, risk retaliation and firing, and most likely end up with token awards that may take more years to collect. And if one case succeeds every ten to fifteen years, so what? It's a cost of doing business, much cheaper than actually bringing women's pay into line with men's.* And it means the power equation will remain intact—one case will usually do *nothing* in the long run to change outcomes for women as a group, or to change the corporate culture that allowed the discrimination to happen in the first place.

Before lasting change can happen, we have to stop believing that it's individual effort alone that gets people to the top, or that individual remedies will be effective. And we have to stop believing that justice in the workplace will win out. Women don't need to become "whiners and victims," but we are indeed fools if we don't recognize that there are institutional factors—built into the system—that make it easier for some people than others. To wit: monolithic networks of individuals *who are in a position to promote others,* workplace

---

*The $54 million that Morgan Stanley agreed to pay in 2004 to settle a sex discrimination case was less than 1 1/2 percent of their net income for one year. In 2004 they could have set aside enough money to pay comparable fines in each of the next sixty-six years and still not show a loss.

policies (or practices) that make it harder for one group to advance over another, or just plain ignorance and inattention on the part of those in charge. Individual effort will get a few women to a few high places. But no amount of *individual* effort will bring women along *as a group* until these things change in a fundamental way. Once we accept this, we can stop blaming ourselves and get out of the "endless improvement" trap. After slightly more than a generation, we need to face the reality that if women could improve themselves into the executive suites, they'd have been the majority at the top long ago. And though laws are a last resort and we need them on the books, they are not likely to be of much practical help to the average working woman.

Augusta National Member Profile
Kenneth Lewis, CEO, Bank of America

When the Augusta National membership list was revealed, Bank of America's CFO, James Hance, was on it. The bank had responded to NCWO's letter questioning Hance's membership with palaver about it being "personal" and assuring us that the company was on both the *Working Mother* and *Fortune* lists as a good company for women. At the height of the controversy, CEO Kenneth Lewis thumbed his nose at women by joining his underling Hance and former Bank of America board member Hootie Johnson as a member at Augusta.

The bank scrambled to save their image with women by granting a sponsor's exemption to Annika Sorenstam to play against the men at the Colonial Golf Tournament. The matchup produced two weeks of international sports headlines and intense worldwide coverage. Lewis went on television to brag about how much money Bank of America was making by sponsoring Sorenstam, even as he fled members of the press asking about his apparent hypocrisy. When they finally caught up with him, "all he could do was babble about some magazine award for diversity," according to one reporter.

In spring 2004, NCWO announced a partnership with the law firm of Mehri & Skalet, litigators of landmark race discrimination cases, to investigate charges of sex discrimination at financial firms, including Bank of America. We asked the companies to prove they had nothing to hide by filling out a questionnaire on pay and promotion, board memberships, and compensation of highest executives by gender. The bank immediately dispatched three senior women to Washington to meet with us to "seek a solution."

After a somewhat uncertain start, the meeting was cordial. The women were sure Kenneth Lewis would agree to resign his membership at Augusta National, as he was a man they knew well, who solidly supported women in the workplace. They went on to say that he would undoubtedly also be willing to announce "a new initiative" on women at Bank of America to remove the bank from scrutiny. As for Hance, he was "on his way out," so his membership would soon become irrelevant.

Because the NCWO chair and vice chair were both leaving for

speeches in China three weeks hence, we asked that they work to secure Lewis's agreement quickly with details to be worked out later. Though we warned them that women in other companies had tried and failed to get their CEOs to resign their membership, they again assured us that Lewis was different and would see it their way. They would get back to us with the good news within days.

Despite numerous follow-up e-mails and calls, we never heard from them again.

The Diversity Dodge

If there was one thing that had become crystal clear from the Augusta controversy it was that corporate America does not respect its female employees, and many have records to prove it. When high-level business leaders show by their actions (or inaction) that sex discrimination is no big deal, it helps to legitimize "a lesser place" for women throughout society. Through the message the Augusta National memberships sent, the CEOs of the largest companies made a mockery of the notion that women are (or will ever be) equals in the workplace. But that doesn't mean they don't try to look like champions of equal opportunity. The most frequent tactic is citing magazine lists and awards for "diversity," coupled with programs that have names such as the GE Women's Network and Women & Company (Citigroup).

> . . . Immelt . . . has loudly pledged to make GE a model of diversity, especially in the senior ranks . . . [Begley] at 32 became the youngest corporate officer in GE history.[71]

> Citigroup has long had strong policies and practices concerning diversity. [The company has been listed as] one of

the top ten Best Companies for Working Mothers . . . and Company of the Year for Latinas to work for in the U.S. (*Latina Style* magazine).[72]

IBM is proud of its long standing commitment to diversity . . . all of our marketing and outreach programs such as our ads in *Working Woman* and *Working Mother* magazines, our support of several of NCWO's member organizations . . .[73]

[Ford Motor Company's] record stands for itself, as evidenced by our selection as one of the 100 Best Companies for Working Mothers.[74]

For 17 years, *Working Mother* magazine has recognized Bank of America . . . We are proud of our legacy, which distinguishes Bank of America as a corporate leader in the area of diversity . . .[75]

Pretend for a minute that you are a parent and your child's school has just been chosen as one of the Top 100 Schools of the Year by two different scholastic magazines. Your school is number 60 out of 100 on the first list, and number 58 on the second. Pretty impressive: not in the top half of the top 100, but still quite good considering the number of schools in the country. Now suppose you learn that the first magazine allowed the school to rate itself by sending in descriptions of academic programs and policies, but the school didn't have to provide any data on performance. A little less impressive. The second magazine did rate the schools on student performance, promotion rates, quality of programs, and learning environment—much more trustworthy, until you take a look at the actual report cards that go with the rankings. You learn that the number-one school on that list has an average grade of only 28 percent, and the last one on the "Top 100" list has a paltry 11 percent average. This puts your kid's school at around 14 percent on a scale of 100. Still impressed?

Obviously you'd be calling the school to see who was running the place, and you'd also wonder what kind of publications would hand out awards on the basis of self-ratings and low performance. Suppose from the phone call you learned that the school employed a vice principal whose main job was not to teach kids or ensure quality programs, but to fill out the forms and provide data to make sure the school was included on as many "best schools" lists as possible, and after that to spend your tax dollars publicizing the awards and placing ads in the magazines that gave them. You'd probably get together with other parents and demand that the vice principal be fired, or at the very least take your child out and put her in a school with some standards and a decent record. And you'd no doubt also have a few choice words for your school board for squandering your tax dollars on the vice principal's position, regardless of what the other schools on the list did. You most certainly would not feel great about the rankings, nor brag to your friends and neighbors about being a parent and taxpayer in such a wonderful school system.

This scenario actually happens again and again in the United States every year, only the awardees are

> The award is merely for performance relative to other companies. If we based it on an external standard that was higher, no company would ever apply.
>
> Robert Bard, founder and editor of *Latina Style* magazine, on his "Best Companies for Latinas" annual award

corporations, not schools. They're ranked by a variety of publications and organizations, and judged on such criteria as "family friendly policies" and "diversity programs." In many cases the companies are required only to submit essays or statements detailing why they deserve the award. Where there is a little more rigor (i.e., actually counting the number of female new-hires or women on the board), the companies with the highest numbers get the awards, even if those numbers are miserable when taken on their own merit.

The Diversity Dodge is the full-grown "bastard child" of laws and requirements instituted in the 1960s and 1970s to increase opportunities for women and minority men in American business. Affirmative action (an executive order, not a law) applies to companies receiving government contracts. It requires that companies doing business with the taxpayers have written affirmative action plans to achieve an employee balance that reflects the *available, qualified* pool of workers in a given area. For example, if local universities are graduating 15 percent females in engineering, a firm could be expected to hire close to that percentage of women when it recruits engineers. Companies must also have "goals and timetables" for achieving the balance they put forth in their plans. Federal contractors are also subject to pay equity audit by the Office of Federal Contract Compliance to make sure there is no pay discrimination against women and minority men. While affirmative action requirements do not apply to companies not doing business with the federal government, antidiscrimination laws do apply. Discrimination in hiring, promotion, and pay is prohibited.

Over the years, companies figured out that one of the best ways to demonstrate compliance was through the invention of programs to prove "good faith." These programs would also

> After seeing the Coca-Cola settlement of $192.5 million for African-American employees who charged racial discrimination (see The Diversity Cola Wars: Pepsi Beats Coke), many corporations want to be proactive and avoid problems before they start. They often start by naming someone, usually a person in human resources, to head their diversity efforts, or by forming a diversity council.
>
> Barbara Frankel, "Diversity 101: A Primer for Beginners," DiversityInc.com, 3/18/2002 © 2004

be a good inoculation against big fines or judgments in lawsuits (we're *trying*), not to mention the tremendous public relations and advertising value. What began as scattered efforts and written policies here and there has now grown into full-blown diversity initiatives, with devoted departments, vice presidents, big budgets, and side industries. Companies have outsourced the "woman and minority problems" to these departments, in some cases augmenting with outside consultants to boost the PR value even higher. All of this is cheaper and easier than actually taking a look at hiring, pay, and promotion on a systematic basis and doing something about inequities when they're found—and they would almost always be found, as national statistics on women's employment and pay relative to men show again and again.

Diversity efforts are like a Potemkin village—a lot seems to be going on, but very little is actually

> They want to beat the sheriff. They don't want the same kind of problems that Coca-Cola had or Texaco had or Denny's had. . . .
>
> David Brown, head of diversity practice at executive recruiter Whitehead Mann. Linda Bean, "Malignant Neglect: Why 'We're Doing the Best We Can' Just Doesn't Cut It Anymore," DiversityInc.com, 1/14/2002 © 2004

happening. Vice presidents for diversity initiatives have been a fixture in corporations for more than a decade. Often a big part of the vice president's job is to work with awarding organizations and publications to get the company on as many "Best" lists as possible. And of course the easiest (and in most cases *only*) way to do that is to spend money on advertising in the awarding publication, underwriting the awards dinner— or both. It makes the company look good to the public, it makes the CEO happy, which in turn makes the VP look good to the CEO. So seemingly everybody wins—never mind that the whole thing is a scam. In the same press release that announced a $54 million settlement with women charging sex discrimination in 2004, Morgan Stanley cited the *Working Mother* "Best Companies for Working Mothers" award as evidence of innocence.

SBC, whose CEO's membership in Augusta National belies any real commitment to women, told Cathy Areu, founder of *Catalina*—a magazine for Hispanic women that gives no awards—that the company only has a budget for magazines that place SBC on lists. "We give 30 percent of our advertising budget to *Fortune,*" the HR manager admitted in May 2003. *Fortune* bypasses their ad agency and notifies SBC directly of their place on the upcoming list, she explained. In turn, the company advertises. When asked which programs the company had created for minorities, the manager said SBC had had too many budget cuts to create programs (SBC does have enough money to sponsor the 2005 Masters Tournament). Another manager told Areu that *Fortune* accepted the questionnaire the company returned without any effort to verify that the information was correct. According to *Fortune,* of the 1,200 questionnaires sent out in 2002, only 134 were returned; the "Best Companies for Minorities" list was compiled from this scant response. SBC placed fourth, while Denny's—a company that had been ranked number one the year before despite an $89,400 fine for violating the civil rights of immigrant workers—placed third.[76]

But what could be called the Diversity Dodge is not just a convenient system like the relationship between a prostitute and a john, where both parties know the rules, both get what they came after, and nobody is hurt in the end. Female employees are hurt because the Diversity Dodge is too often a substitute for real action when it comes to programs and policies that produce results. The word *diversity* itself is often a cover for allowing companies to lump women with men of color. It is impossible to tell whether women are advancing separately from minority men, or how minority women are doing when compared to white women. Since the rankings are for the most part meaningless anyway, this may not be much of a loss.

Awards announcements and "Best" lists are just the tip of the iceberg in what has become a multimillion-dollar industry. The Diversity Dodge serves everyone concerned, except the people it ought to benefit—those who work for the corporations, particularly women. It's a simple model, and it's no surprise that it's too often driven by money on one side (the awarders) and dishonesty on the other (the awardees). Here's how it works: A magazine decides to construct a list of the best companies for fill-in-the-blank: women, Hispanics, Asians, minorities in general. Companies apply for the awards through processes that can range from a one-page form or three-page essay to exhaustive questionnaires about hiring, retention, board membership, supplier relationships, child care and leave policies, flextime, and retirement plans. But just because a questionnaire is exhaustive doesn't mean the rankings it produces mean anything. In fact, it often seems that the length and breadth of the forms is a substitute for real rigor in evaluating the information. The more data you gather, the easier it is to cherry pick those pieces that fit your goal. In the end, the process is akin to awarding tenure at a university: If the committee wants to promote you, it can always find a reason in the material you were asked to submit, and if it wants to deny you, there's always enough material to do that too.

In the Diversity Dodge, the companies that buy the most advertising or contribute the most to an "awards" dinner always end up with the best rankings, no matter the process used to get them there. If it's an essay or "employee survey," where the company usually picks the respondents, it's easy, because there are no objective criteria at all. If the process does involve a long questionnaire with lots of data, then the pieces that fit the end goal (a jazzy-sounding new diversity initiative) can be highlighted, and the not-so-good factors (the fact that women aren't advancing as fast as men) can be ignored.

> I don't actually know how we got the awards [for best companies for women]. I just read it in our public relations statements.
>
> Sherry Lui, General Counsel, Motorola China, 5/24/2004

Here's how a typical award works, according to Erin Martin, application coordinator for the Ivy Group, a public relations firm that handles the Diversity Innovator's Award for the Women's Business Center. First, the "data" are gathered. This is usually done via a questionnaire or essay process, in this case described openly as a "self-evaluation." Other awards the firms have received are also part of the process. This leads to a strange form of self-perpetuating validation. For example, having made the *Working Mother* magazine "Best Companies for Working Mothers" or the *Fortune* "Best Companies for Minorities" lists will count for other awards, even if those lists are based on very loose criteria or are an outright quid quo pro for advertising dollars. (In 2003 the *Working Mother* list included Morgan Stanley, a company that was being sued by the EEOC for sex discrimination, and whose CEO, not surprisingly, was a member of Augusta National, as were the CEOs of ten other companies on the list.)* The companies are then rated by a panel of judges, sometimes including diversity consultants and principals of the public relations firm, but most often it's personnel at the awarding organization. Companies are notified of their award or list placement well in advance of the gala, so they can "plan for" the event. This usually means magazine advertising, underwriting the awards announcement gala, and program advertisements. Considerable media outreach is also done to get the company in the news for being honored. In the case of

---

*Awarding organizations can be quite disingenuous in justifying their selections. NCWO met with *Working Mother* editor Carol Evans in 2003 to discuss why the magazine would give awards to companies whose CEOs were engaging in behavior directly contradictory to the spirit of their awards (membership in all male clubs where business is done, and sexual harassment as charged by the EEOC). Evans excused the 2003 Morgan Stanley award by saying *Working Mother* did not consider "pending lawsuits" even if they were initiated by the government. The next year, a question about policies surrounding executive memberships at discriminatory clubs was added to the *Working Mother* questionnaire, specifically mentioning Augusta National. But *Working Mother* did not use the information as a disqualifying factor. When Morgan Stanley women were awarded $54 million in a settlement on the sex discrimination charges in 2004, Evans said the company would still make the list because "they agreed to some good things in the settlement."

Fortune, it's all advertising and publicity, as there is no companion event.

Magazines and awarding organizations vary in how blatant they are about the arrangements. Some, like *Hispanic Network Magazine,* openly tell potential advertisers that they can buy "Corporate Diversity Advertising" and get name recognition in the year-end issue featuring "Top Companies Making a Difference." Most go through some motions to make the lists look legitimate—an application process, so-called judging, and outreach to the winners in plenty of time to complete financial transactions associated with the lists. *Latina Style,* a magazine touted often in company press releases and diversity literature, uses a survey with general questions about company policies on such topics as family leave, child care, and flextime, along with specific questions about the number of Hispanic women in top job categories. When the list comes out, a careful reading shows that actual numbers are included only when they look good—usually one or two of the fifty companies, with data only for all women or all minorities, not Latinas specifically. The remaining forty-nine awards are by scatter shooting, counting a program here, a benefit there, to give all fifty com-

> [Motorola CEO] Galvin does not hesitate to accept awards from organizations like the Business Women's Network in recognition of his "commitment" to "diversity" at Motorola. Would Motorola contract with an organization that excludes women? Would Motorola exclude women from its senior ranks and board? . . . Mr. Galvin is an unrepentant member at Augusta.
>
> Lester Munson, "When It Comes to Equality, Golfing CEOs Are Duffers," *Crain's Chicago Business,* 3/10/2003

panies something to brag about. The vast majority of the fifty honored companies advertise in the magazine. If they don't, they often mysteriously disappear from the list the next year.

While not every single award or "best" list is tainted, most are, even the ones that come from organizations and publications whose goal is to advance women. Catalyst, by their own description the "premier nonprofit research and advisory organization working to advance women in business," is well respected in the business world and the nonprofit world. But it doesn't take a very deep scratch on the surface to uncover troubling information about the organization's structure and award system. In 2004, the Catalyst board of directors included Jeffrey Immelt, CEO of General Electric, Christopher Galvin, immediate past CEO of Motorola, and William B. Harrison, CEO of JPMorgan Chase. Their Chairman Emeritus is John Bryan, retired CEO of Sara Lee Corporation. All members of Augusta National. Though their club memberships had been public for more than a year, Catalyst had not seen fit to address the issue and denied even knowing about it in a meeting with NCWO prior to their 2004 awards. The Catalyst board also included John Mack, CEO of Credit Suisse, the man who reportedly dressed down JPMorgan Chase CFO Dina Dublon for challenging her CEO's membership.

The 2004 Catalyst award went to three companies—headlined by GE, lauded for its General Electric Women's Network, formed in 1998 to "cultivate women leaders." But as Ross Perot used to say, the devil is in the details. If you read to the bottom of the congratulatory paragraph from Catalyst, you learned that executive band women were only 21 percent, 14 percent of senior executive band employees were female, and a measly 13 percent of the 173 corporate officers at GE were female. The reason given by Catalyst for honoring such pitiful numbers was that they were up from 18 percent, 9 percent, and 5 percent respectively since 1998. Any school would be given a failing grade, not an award, if it turned in such a poor performance.

Now, look closer. Besides the still very low numbers, we see that the glass ceiling is still in place at GE. As women climb the ranks, their numbers go down, even in the "new and improved" environment that Catalyst is awarding. At this rate it will take approximately fifty-four more years for women to reach parity at the executive level, forty-two years to reach parity at the senior executive level, and twenty-four years to get even at the corporate officer level. That's a whole career in anybody's book, and that's assuming the quota system for keeping the number of women below a certain level doesn't kick in somewhere along the road to improvement. One more thing—Catalyst itself found GE below average for the Fortune 500 the year before. The contribution to Catalyst that companies make as board members is somewhere between $25,000 and $50,000 a year, not counting the contribution to the event where the award is handed out. A cheap enough date, considering the full-page ad Catalyst runs in *The New York Times* praising the awardees, and the fact that awardees now have the imprimatur of a "premier" organization devoted to women and business, which they can use extensively in promotion and public relations materials.

And use the awards they do. GE prominently displayed the Catalyst logo on its website after the award, and so-called "honors" are routinely touted in press releases, advertising, and public relations efforts by virtually all of the companies involved. Citigroup publishes a slick "Diversity Annual Report," with all their awards prominently displayed on the inside back cover, opposite their "Workforce Information Report." The report is a chart with raw numbers of employees by gender, race, and broad job category. Once again doing the math, we learn that Citigroup's 2003 "Best Companies for Latinas" award, conferred by *Latina Style* magazine, was based on a total workforce participation of only 5.6 percent Latinas at the company—the clear majority (72 percent) of them in the clerical pool. A mere 2 percent of the revenue-producing sales jobs were held by Latinas.

The Diversity Dodge has spawned side industries dedicated to helping companies find the places that give diversity awards and connecting vice presidents of diversity to awarding organizations. The Business Women's Network (BWN), a division of iVillage, publishes a biannual *Best of the Best: Corporate Awards for Diversity and Women,* a thick book detailing which awards and lists are available, the criteria, the associated event with dates, and most importantly, the public relations promotions that are provided by the awarding organizations. The research for the book allows BWN to produce yet another list, called the "Best of the Best." It's basically a "Best List" for getting on the most "Best Lists." For 2003–2004, Verizon placed first because the company made seventeen lists. SBC was fifth, with twelve lists under its belt.

The Business Women's Network has also created a "unique membership service" called Diversity Best Practices (DBP), which is a "one stop service for diversity and benchmarking." BWN/DBP has its own corporate CEO Leadership Award, which is handed out at a multimillion-dollar Diversity and Women Leadership Summit & Gala. No one knows the exact criteria for selection, but the list is long on "supporting" things like diversity goals, mentoring, and "endorsement of

In 2002, the Augusta National membership list became public after the Business Women's Network Diversity Award recipients were chosen, but before the event took place. Two of the awardees, William B. Harrison (JPMorgan Chase) and Christopher Galvin (Motorola), were exposed as members of Augusta National. BWN had to backtrack with the media and assert that the awards were really "for the company," since these men were engaging in behavior directly contrary to the purpose of the award. NCWO used the fact of the award announcement to point out the hypocrisy of the two CEOs, and members of the media tried to goad us into picketing the event. We declined. BWN had no way to know about the Augusta memberships prior to choosing Harrison and Galvin, because the list had been secret. We saw no reason to divert attention from the sex discrimination and hypocrisy by fighting publicly with another women's group.

No Augusta National members have been included in the awards since. It is unclear whether the decision was made because BWN President Edie Fraser was offended by the idea that CEOs would belong to a club where business is clearly done and the women she champions are excluded (she told NCWO she was "totally on your side—but I've got a business to run"), or whether the embarrassment of 2002 was not worth the contribution the winning companies made. Regardless, BWN did the right thing.

diversity sponsorships and support for diversity advertising." No actual data on employee diversity, such as pay and promotion statistics, are required. Ironically, the nine corporate CEO recipients of the 2003 awards were all white men. BWN/DBP "worked with" the magazine *Diversity Journal* (which itself gives awards) to get all nine on that month's cover under the banner "The New Face of Corporate Diversity." It was a stunning cover.

Unlike the publications whose only diversity activities are list production, awards, and resultant advertising sales, organizations such as BWN, Catalyst, and DiversityInc. (which gives its own awards and sells ads in its magazine to the recipients) also sell diversity services. They have solid information to give employers about the value of diversity programs, how to move women up in the organization, and the relationship between the number of female employees and the bottom line. They even provide high-quality consulting services to companies that genuinely want to improve. It's just that these services are secondary to the primary goals of high-profile list placement (and "silver bullet" lawsuit protection) on the corporate side, and financial gain through ads and contributions on the awarding organization side.

Even organizations with *no* financial incentive to include a given company in rankings count tainted data in their rating systems. KLD Consulting is a company that does the research for the Domini 400 Social Index (an investor service) and provides data for *Business Ethics* magazine to use in constructing its "100 Best Corporate Citizens" list. If a company makes the *Working Mother* list, it gets positive points in the KLD evaluation. But KLD does not have the resources to independently verify a company's performance on any of the criteria used by *Working Mother,* or even see the completed forms. Simply appearing on the final list is enough—even if *Working Mother* missed something or evaluated its winners with one eye on ad revenue. This, along with lumping women and minority men into a single "diversity" category, contributes to the "too much for too little" phenomenon, since companies with what could only be considered poor performance when held to an objective standard can often make a list because they're better than their peers. In KLD's case, having no woman on the board or in top management would not necessarily disqualify a company, since the score given out is for "diversity" in general and includes data on minority contracting and other factors that could outweigh the exclusion of women.

The question that must be asked is why any employer should be rewarded for poor performance, even if it is the best of the worst. Here's the real bottom line: If companies can get away with creating programs, diversity councils, diversity training, fancy mission statements, and great-sounding initiatives and get an award without actually having to improve performance, it's cheaper and easier than solving problems. And there is a whole industry out there to help them do just that.

Take the equal pay problem, which polls number one with women in survey after survey about workplace concerns. By "equal pay": Some women know they are being paid less than men for doing the same job. Some women know the job titles are different but the work is just as demanding, and the pay scales are way out of whack. Yet none of the list builders or award givers looks at pay in a way that is meaningful to the average working woman. The toughest question asked is usually how many of the top 50 or 100 earners are female. If 10 percent of the top earners are female, the company is probably going to get a top award, because 10 percent tends to be better than most other companies. On the other hand, if those high-earning females are like women at the lower ranks, they're likely earning 75 percent of what the male earners in their peer group are paid—clear evidence of sex discrimination (as if 90 percent of the top earners being male weren't enough). But nobody asks, and the companies wouldn't answer if they did. Not insignificantly, in many companies you can be fired for discussing pay data with coworkers.

Creating programs runs a close second to chasing diversity

awards when it comes to ways companies try to look good without actually having to address the glass ceiling and pay inequities directly. General Electric can serve as a good example. The company has "programs" to prove they're dedicated to fairness in the workplace. Besides the Women's Network, which "provides mentoring and coaching" and allows women to "share information on job opportunities," there's the African-American Forum, where "employees from similar cultures . . . learn from the mistakes and successes of others"; the Asian-Pacific American Forum, which provides "career development and a support network for APAF professionals"; the Hispanic Forum, which offers a "system based on individual self-help and networking" to develop and retain Hispanic talent.

It's easy to spot the three prominent aspects of these networks and similar targeted programs: (1) They are designed so that employees can talk to one another in affinity groups, dividing them from other groups that could be natural allies in changing company culture and confronting the practices that keep the glass ceiling in place—an "us against them" model; (2) From this model flows the notion (very often reality) that there are going to be a certain number of slots at each higher level for "women and minorities" and they must compete with one another to get those few slots (reserving *all* of the other slots as a pool for white men); (3) By creating subgroups around self-help, networking, and mentoring with one another, the company is creating an atmosphere and expectation that responsibility for advancing women or minority men depends on employees helping each other, not with those who have the power to change processes that enforce the status quo. This could be labeled the "keep 'em divided and talking to one another, so they won't complain to us" model of management.

Augusta National Member Profile
Philip Purcell, CEO, Morgan Stanley

Philip Purcell has been CEO of Morgan Stanley since 1997. Purcell's interlocking relationships with other Augusta National members are extensive. He sits on the AMR board with Edward Brennan, and the Committee to Encourage Corporate Philanthrophy with fifteen other members.

Under Purcell, Morgan Stanley has settled claims for financial conflicts of interest, and race, sex, and sexual orientation discrimination, paying out millions while denying guilt. William Donaldson, chairman of the Securities and Exchange Commission, publicly rebuked Purcell in 2003 for saying he did not see anything in a settlement over conflicts of interest that should concern retail investors about Morgan Stanley. Donaldson wrote, "Your reported comments evidence a troubling lack of contrition and lead me to wonder about Morgan Stanley's commitment to compliance with the letter and spirit of the law and the high standards of conduct all investors have a right to expect from their brokerage firms."

Under Purcell, Morgan Stanley brought criminal charges against Christian Curry after firing him for alleged expense account abuse when his picture appeared in a gay magazine. Manhattan prosecutors dropped the charges after they discovered the company paid ten thousand dollars to a confidential informant for a tip that led to Curry's arrest. In court, assistant district attorney LeRoy Frazer said Morgan Stanley officials paid the informant and also "withheld . . . information" about it. Curry sued for race and sexual orientation discrimination. The case ended in September 2000 when a settlement was reached. There was no admission of fault by either party, but a "donation" of $1 million by Morgan Stanley to the National Urban League was part of the deal.

Purcell was extraordinarily resistant to settling sex discrimination charges brought against the company by the EEOC on behalf of Alison Schieffelin, a former convertible-bond salesperson who was fired after she complained of discrimination. Having failed to settle even when summoned by the judge for a three-hour one-on-one session with the EEOC lawyer in 2003, Purcell was personally involved in negotiations when the company agreed to settle with Schieffelin for $12 million minutes before the trial began in

2004. Schieffelin's statement at the time the case was filed said in part:

"The campaign of retaliation that Morgan Stanley launched against me was designed not only to punish me but also to scare other women who might dare to complain of discrimination . . . Morgan Stanley destroyed my career. . . . And the retaliation that I endured has had the effect, and I believe the intent, of sending a loud message to women that if they complain, they too will be diminished. . . . Morgan Stanley had no interest in fixing the problem of gender discrimination."

On Wall Street in December 2003, unemployment was rising while year-end bonuses made headlines. The biggest reported bonus went to Philip Purcell, who took in $12 million. In New York there were reports of fancy restaurants with waiting lines and President Bush said, "This economy of ours is strong and it is getting stronger." Purcell, along with fellow Augusta National members George David, James Hance, and Edward Whitacre Jr., was listed as a "Ranger" for the 2004 George W. Bush campaign. To be so listed, an individual had to have raised at least $200,000 for the candidate.

Old Barriers, New Solutions

Recognizing Barriers

The pay gap is probably the most misunderstood statistic in the gender/workplace dialogue; given today's reality, it's actually worse than it looks. Not all of the difference in earnings between women and men working full-time year-round (23 percent) is due to overt discrimination, but experts agree that a little less than half of it can't be explained any other way. A big part of wage disparities for this group comes from sex segregation of jobs where the "women's jobs" pay less. But once we leave the full-time, year-round population, the unyielding workplace model is a formidable factor. For women who drop out of the workforce even for a year, the penalty is a whopping 32 percent of total earnings for the next *fifteen years*,

> So who wins? Corporate America wins, and wins big. By suppressing working women's wages, they maximize their profits, pay less to the government in taxes and less to pension plans . . . the most lucrative corporate welfare plan ever.
>
> "Why Women Don't Deserve Equal Pay!" Paul E. Almeida, Department of Public Employees, AFL-CIO, 2003

and it goes up to 46 percent and 56 percent for two and three years off respectively.[77] This means that for a woman making $35,000, dropping out for a single year will cost a minimum of $168,000, not counting inflation or raises.

Closing the pay gap has implications far beyond boosting incomes in two-earner families. Higher wages for mothers who are sole breadwinners would bring families out of poverty and give their children a more equal start in life. Higher pay would bring single female workers into the same income bracket as their male counterparts; parity at the beginning of a career, when females are still hired at lower salaries than males, would translate into higher lifetime earnings, a higher standard of living, and a higher contribution to the national tax base. (There is a reason why marketers routinely target gay male households—single males living together have the highest disposable income of any group.)

There is a less obvious reason for closing the pay gap, but it ultimately could have the most enduring effects. It would go a long way toward equalizing the status between men and women in families, and over time it would affect fundamental decisions about the division of labor, sex roles, and who is "entitled" to what. We talked in "The Deep Divide" (see page 15) about the ingrained belief that the female gender has less status and is therefore seen as less important in society. Historically, the pay gap is a *result* of this belief ("women's jobs" are worth less, and women don't "need" the same pay as men), but now the pay gap also *perpetuates* it.

People live out results of the pay gap's reinforcement of gender superiority every day. If a child is sick or a repairman must be met, who is going to stay home? The person who loses the least in pay or career advancement possibilities. If a transfer comes up, whose job takes precedence? The one with the higher pay and the most upward mobility. Granted, the person staying home or turning down the move is sometimes the male, but in 99 percent of the cases it's the female, because she makes less. This could be because she merely has a job, whereas he has a career, since both know at the outset that he will go further. So the pay gap both reinforces and perpetuates itself—and the gender superiority stereotypes along with it— entrenching systemic discrimination.

No one should believe that we would have true family equality if the salary disparities were erased tomorrow. "Father knows best" is too ingrained in our psyches. But after a generation of family decisions guided by a balanced family economic equation, attitudes would surely follow. Men say they want more time at home—pay equity for women would free them to pursue that goal.

It's a mystery why lack of child care, so persistently mentioned as a dominant factor in the "opting out" stories, is not viewed as another form of systemic discrimination, demanding more than individual solutions. In speeches, I am fond of saying that if Tinker Bell visited the planet and sprinkled her magic dust some night when we were all asleep, and when we woke up all the kids on earth "belonged" to the men, we'd have a child care center on every corner before noon.

While there are certainly organized groups who have been working for years to get some kind of universal, government-funded or workplace-provided child care, parents as a group have not mobilized. They've apparently bought in to the idea that "the personal is personal." If you can't find good child care you just live in the wrong neighborhood, don't look hard enough, or are just personally unlucky enough not to have a job that pays enough to afford it. Besides, families (mothers) need to be responsible for their kids. The idea that there is a public responsibility for child care, just like free public schools—which were once highly controversial—seems an alien concept. And whether we like it or not, working women are bearing the brunt. Families, because of the pay gap and those ingrained attitudes, still view women as primarily responsible for the kids. Of course, single mothers have no choice. (It should not go unremarked that a fair number of women have custody because courts buy in to the stereotype too, even sometimes to the detriment of children.)

Close your eyes and envision a working world where child care is of good quality, affordable, and available at work or as part of the public school system. Then the major decision might be who dropped off or picked up the kids, not who works and who doesn't, and at what job. Of course, families who could afford it might still opt for a stay-at-home parent, but if the pay gap were erased that parent wouldn't automatically be the mother.

Americans are working more hours now than they did a generation ago, as real incomes have fallen. The forty-hour workweek in the United States is largely disappearing, and it has been long gone for any job that can remotely be classified as "managerial" or "professional," or where the salary is high enough to exempt the employee from overtime pay requirements (only $23,660 per year in 2004). A company culture of long work hours most obviously creates a burden for those who must leave the job before the day care center closes (mostly women). Even where kids are not a factor, killer hours also disadvantage anyone who just doesn't want to work sixty hours a week to curry favor with the boss or get the key account. But since people without outside mandatory responsibilities are mostly male—they *can* work those sixty hours even if they don't want to—men once again gain a competitive advantage over women.

A workplace structure that demands inhumane and unreasonable hours, the legacy of a past when work was designed for men with stay-at-home wives, is, simply put, another form of systemic discrimination. The fact that women are free to "compete" in this time-skewed environment does not change the fact that longer hours have a disparate impact on women's ability to get ahead on an even basis with men. *It's the environment itself that's the problem.* And it goes without saying that the long-hours treadmill has a negative impact on quality of life, not only for women, but for men trapped in the "be there or lose out" environment. (Of course, if you claw your way to the very top, hours are no longer a problem. You "work" on the golf course or at the Olympics with other CEOs like Kenneth Chenault of American Express, as the AMEX employee manual patiently explains.[78] At the other end of the scale—low-wage hourly work—you're not there to get ahead of the competition. You're there because you need the extra hours' pay.)

There is no question that today's workplace is too demanding—for everyone. Globalization has meant more job insecurity, and the information revolution has

> The truth about women in power is that our status has changed but not the institutions and policymaking structures that make up the world in which we must function. To end discrimination, it is not enough to gain a place in the existing system. We need to *change the system.*
>
> Harriet Woods, "The Unplayable Field," presentation for Oxford Round Table, 8/11/2003

meant longer hours on the job and twenty-four-hour accessibility. We need solutions so that women (and a few men) are not forced to derail career progress or leave work altogether due to family obligations. But more crucially, solutions must be crafted for women who don't leave work (by far the majority) but stay and strive, either because they must (just like the men) or because they want and are entitled to work outside the home and find it personally rewarding (just like the men).

It's true that many large corporations have "family-friendly" policies affecting the ability to take time off, such as flextime, personal leave for school events, and in rarer cases, job sharing. The problem with family-friendly policies is that while on the surface they are gender neutral, in reality they are used very little by men. This means two things: (1) If women take advantage of programs allowing shorter hours or more time off, they're building their own "mommy track"—fewer and slower promotions and lower pay. (2) Men who stay at work longer hours and never take off for the kids' parent-teacher meetings or an elderly parent's illness will also benefit from the perception that they're "more serious" workers and more committed to their careers. If men took advantage of family policies as often as women, and it was seen as "normal" for them to do so, then the genders would benefit equally (or be equally disadvantaged, if you want to look at it that way). It is obvious that this discussion is much less relevant for both women and men who have zero family responsibilities, but the majority of workers are married and a vast number have children younger than eighteen. As longevity increases, even more workers will face time off to care for elderly parents at some point in their careers.

Crafting Solutions
Positive Momentum Laws

Would new laws help? You bet. But not if the new laws were cast in the same old complaint-driven, unworkable paradigm, like the proposals to step up enforcement that are perennials on Capitol Hill. We need laws that create *positive momentum,* not just negative sanctions. Think about it—the few laws we already have that translate directly to better outcomes for workers are not complaint driven—they create positive obligations. Minimum wage, family leave, and mandatory overtime pay after a certain number of hours all have this in common. The employer is directed by the government to *do something*—pay a mandated wage or grant a benefit—not to just theoretically conform to a prohibition and wait to get sued if they don't.

A great example of a positive momentum law is the pay equity statute in Ontario, Canada, passed in 1988. The Pay Equity Act requires that jobs in workplaces with ten or more employees be evaluated. Work mostly or traditionally done by women must be compared to work mostly or traditionally done by men. For each job, employers must look at the skill, effort, responsibility, and working conditions, and give the job a *value* based on those factors. If a discrepancy is found based on this value, the pay rate for the job must be adjusted, even if the titles and duties are quite different. For example, if the analysis reveals that secretarial work has the same value as package shipping but the secretarial job category is payed less overall, compensation is adjusted upward. No individual's pay can be lowered to achieve pay equity, and adjustments can be made gradually (1 percent of annual payroll) so that employers will not be unduly burdened. The Ontario statute continues to be recognized as one of the world's most effective laws in redressing the wage gap. The pay gap has decreased by 25 percent since the law was passed, and women are still receiving pay adjustments.

California passed another positive momentum law—the first paid family leave law in the country—in 2001. Beginning on July 1, 2004, nearly all non-governmental employees in California became eligible to receive paid family leave through a state-administered program (State Disability Insurance). Working Californians can take job-protected paid family leave to care for a seriously ill family member or to bond with a new child, and the worker can collect as much as 55 percent of their salary, up to a maximum of $728 per week. Workers pay for the program through payroll deductions averaging only $27 per year. It's too early to tell how broad the effect will be, but there is no question that with this benefit more workers will opt to take leave. Since research indicates that lack of pay replacement has been a particular barrier for male workers because they are the higher earners, it's a safe bet that a good number of new California leave-takers will be male.

Some areas, especially the problems of poor women (and men) working for hourly wages without benefits, have historically been attacked by positive momentum laws designed to lift people out of poverty. But the progress has stalled. The impending crisis of economic inequality resulting from a permanent population of working poor that now approaches 25 percent of the workforce cannot be solved in a few paragraphs. (The working poor [less than $9.04 per hour] are mostly female [58 percent], mostly white [58 percent], and mostly high school educated or higher [77 percent].)[79] Economists are increasingly alarmed and continue to advocate structural, public solutions.

Raising the minimum wage, expanding the Earned Income Tax Credit (EITC), increasing child care subsidies for those who cycle on and off public assistance, and solving the lack of health insurance would each make a positive difference.[80] But without politicians committed to change, these solutions are still just words on paper.

Positive momentum laws work. But let's face it, even the working poor are unlikely to get new laws anytime soon, and the probability of new employment legislation aimed above the poverty line is even more remote. The last significant workplace legislation was the *unpaid* Family and Medical Leave Act of 1993 (if you work for a large employer). And it took almost ten years of hard lobbying by women's groups to pass even that. Bills to narrow the pay gap have been languishing in Congress in one form or another since the original Equal Pay Act passed in 1963. So even though legislative solutions are still badly needed, there's not much promise on the horizon. With the ascendancy of conservative dogma about women's workplace inequities being the result of private choices (just read the magazines), many lawmakers no longer even believe we need the laws we've got. Of course, more female lawmakers would help. Women—who are likely to care more than men about these problems regardless of party—still make up only 13 percent of Congress. At the present rate, it will take three hundred more years to reach parity with their male colleagues.

The Positive Momentum Strategy for Companies

We know that most non-government fixes can realistically apply only to workers who are not on the very bottom rungs.

But even at the bottom, while there is no law that says people must be paid more than subsistence wages or that benefits should be available to every worker, *there is also no law that says this couldn't happen if employers were willing to make change on their own.* Take Wal-Mart, the nation's largest employer, with a 72 percent female workforce. Males are 85.7 percent of the managers, while 92.5 percent of the lowest-paid workers (cashiers) are female. It's no surprise that women are suing the company in the largest class action sex discrimination case in history. High premiums and deductibles keep more than two-thirds of Wal-Mart workers from participating in the company health plan, which extracts a much-higher-than-average contribution from employees.

The five members of the Walton family, owners of Wal-Mart, hold positions four to eight on the *Fortune* list of the four hundred richest Americans, with assets of $102.5 billion. If they gave up just *1 percent* of that in the form of higher wages for their workers, it would be enough to provide affordable health care for their associates.[81] If they were willing to go as high as 2 cents on the dollar, they could also raise the wages of their approximately 1.2 million U.S. workers by $3 per hour—enough to lift many of them above the poverty line. If this is too much to ask of the Wal-Mart owners, maybe we could all pay 2 cents more for those plastic doll buggies, neon-colored flip-flops, or the latest anti-woman DVD or video game. But even if we did, it's almost a sure bet that the Waltons wouldn't give those extra pennies to the workers. Of course, Wal-Mart is allowed to seek a fair profit, as are all businesses. But the key word is *fair.* If corporations are entitled to the *most profit they can possibly make,* we should go ahead and abolish the corruption laws, the minimum wage, and repeal our employment discrimination laws—or maybe just go back to slavery and forget about paying workers altogether.

When being denied a living wage and basic benefits is not the issue, more creative solutions are possible. And again, they don't take government mandates. What they do take is commitment on the part of management and the board of directors to truly make change, not just put in policies that look good on paper or disproportionately affect one group if they're actually implemented. Make no mistake, corporate culture matters. If management's attitude is that men really own the jobs and are better at them, while women are really outsiders who must only be let in at the margins, the long-term outlook in that company is poor at best. And who is supposed to be the embodiment and the chief spokesman for corporate culture and values? The CEO and, to a lesser extent, the senior executives and the board of directors. Corporate culture is one place where the "trickle down" theory works—either overtly or covertly. That's why a "good old boys" cult at the top translates into fewer opportunities for women, pay imbalances, and even looking the other way on sexual harassment.

Even if management is committed to women's advancement, without firm written policies, the commitment could last only until the next management shake-up or CEO retirement. As we've seen, most large firms have a lot of policies and they look pretty good on paper—dedication to equal opportunity, opposition to discrimination in any form, programs that foster inclusion, a commitment to being "family-friendly," and on and on *ad nauseam*. But unless the CEO and top management are committed to outcomes, policy alone is meaningless. And since the CEO is seen as the embodiment of company principles, what he does is emulated down the line.

Many women told us that the attitude conveyed by their CEO's Augusta National membership trickled down to frontline management. As a woman at Prudential said to me, "Why do we have to go to all these 'diversity' trainings when the CEO does something like this? It affects the way other men act in the company too."

Policy is also meaningless without measurement. As we've seen with the Diversity Dodge, words aren't much good without some mechanism to make sure the goals are implemented. Even implementation may not be sufficient (e.g., diversity seminars may be held regularly or affinity groups may be formed, but promotion rates for women and minority men don't budge). The only thing that really counts is whether these policies and programs produce the results they were designed to achieve. How do you know if that's happening? The same way you know whether the company is making a profit. You look at the numbers.

No amount of antidiscrimination directives, diversity initiatives, or slick brochures featuring women workers can take the place of institutional systems of accountability for achieving results. Managers are held accountable for sales numbers, CEOs are held accountable for stock prices, and boards are (sort of) held accountable for financial malfeasance. Why, if companies believe so strongly in women workers (as they claim), is there no accountability for retention and promotion of women? And if the company cares enough to put policies on paper, shouldn't it care enough to monitor compliance?

The fact that CEOs who hold membership in Augusta National are not even held accountable to their own boards for policies against supporting discriminatory organizations or entertaining clients at discriminatory venues is a salient example.* Consider the complaint filed by the EEOC against Morgan Stanley that was settling for $54 million in 2004. Among other things, the complaint cited client entertainment at golf courses and strip clubs where women were excluded.[82] Is it an accident that Philip Purcell, the CEO, is a member of Augusta National, a club that proudly discriminates against women? That membership, even in the face of national controversy, embarrassment for the company, and the formal opposition of women's groups, civil rights groups, and socially responsible investment firms, says a lot about how the company culture is defined: *Sex discrimination is not serious, keeping women out is okay.* That's why the Augusta National controversy goes far beyond the links, to the very top of companies that not only control women's work lives, but set the standard in corporate America. It is emblematic of how the management of most companies *really* views women.

Even if a company does have an explicit policy and adheres to it in a technical sense, company culture can get around it unless the CEO sets the right example. And too often he sets the wrong one. Companies like Morgan Stanley, whose managers have entertained clients at strip clubs (which after all admit women), or Wal-Mart, where management

---

*The Augusta National controversy uncovered a lot of weakness and hypocrisy in this area. Some firms, like IBM, have such a policy but allow top management to ignore it. Some others, like Bank of America, had such prohibitions in the past, but apparently dropped them by allowing the CEO to be an Augusta member. The Bank of America policy on exclusionary club memberships for top executives was cited in the legal briefs as exemplary during the New York Club litigation in the 1980s. Twenty years later, the bank's CEO, Kenneth Lewis, joined Augusta National at the height of the controversy, and the bank archivist refused to produce the policy, citing "confidentiality."

meetings have been held at Hooters,[83] are not as rare as we'd like to think. But even if it doesn't go that far, football games, boxing tournaments, fishing and golf trips (one woman was left behind when she refused to share a condo with three male colleagues), and similar client entertainment venues are reinforcers of the idea that women don't belong, or, if they must be included, are "fifth wheels."

We need some new quotas that work as well as the old quotas. Every time women suggest that they should be represented in leadership in proportion to their numbers in a given institution, they are accused of being "quota queens." Yet there has been a very effective quota system in corporate America since the industrial revolution, when women's cheap labor was recruited at the bottom to support the men who ruled at the top. The present quotas say something like, "Women can have all the lower-level jobs we can fill, but we have an 89 percent quota for men in management and a 99 percent quota for men in CEO positions." This needs to change, and it needs to change in a concrete way—not with general policies and platitudes that don't translate to action. Under Al Neuharth, *USA Today* made progress on parity for minorities and women part of the management review for every departmental manager. If the CEO is serious about it, managers can be held accountable by tying part of their compensation to goals for women's progress in the company, just as they're held accountable for production or sales quotas.

We know the pay gap consistently polls near the top when women are asked about workplace concerns, and we've seen how closing it could eventually affect family decisions about who does what and when, eventually helping to change the equality equation in families. But we also know that short of completely overhauling our existing laws and creating strong new ones besides, we're not going to bring women's pay into line through government action. Companies that really want to even out pay disparities can do it on their own, with a pretty simple plan. They can perform gender equity audits of their own workforce practices, just like they perform financial audits. Nonfinancial audits are not a new idea—social responsibility audits briefly gained some traction in the 1970s when companies were trying to paint themselves "green" on a wave of environmentalism.[84]

And what would a gender equity audit look like? It could take many forms—there are a number of templates ranging from the very simple to complicated and lengthy. All are designed to answer a few basic questions about pay and promotion, and to highlight deficiencies in company policy or practice that may be leading to pay gaps and glass ceilings. It is important that gender equity audits be about *females only*—include race and ethnicity only if female race and ethnicity is broken out separately from males. Race and ethnicity data should not be included if males in those totals are lumped in, as is often the case, because totals are distorted. If "women and minorities" are one category, a high number of minority males in management may obscure a paucity of women, and there is no way to know whether the minority women are counted twice to make the overall totals look better.

A BASIC GENDER EQUITY AUDIT

- Company-wide statistics on pay grade by gender, with averages for women and men at each pay grade for each job category

- Number of promotions by gender, with average salary grade improvement by percentage and amount

- Compensation of the 150 highest-paid individuals (including not only base salary, but stock options, bonuses, and other forms of special compensation) by gender

- Stock option distribution by gender and number of shares

- Number of new hires by gender, with pay averages at each hiring grade

- Number of layoffs by gender and job category

- Turnover statistics by job category and gender

- Number of individuals taking family leave by gender

- Attendance at company-paid seminars and/or continuing education hours by gender

- Number of female and male candidates interviewed for board openings

- New board members by gender

- Company policy and procedures for enforcement against holding official events or functions or client entertainment at venues that discriminate against women

- Company policy and procedures for enforcement against support of organizations that discriminate against women through event sponsorships, philanthropic gifts, program advertising, and the like

- Company policy on executive expenses (such as membership dues, travel, housing, client development, or events) at or in conjunction with venues that discriminate against women

- Actual expenditures—either direct payments, or direct or indirect reimbursement of executive expenses (such as membership dues, travel, housing, client development, advertising, or events)—at or in conjunction with venues that bar women, some or all of the time

- Actual amounts—either direct payments, or direct or indirect reimbursement of executive expenses (such as membership dues, travel, housing, client development, advertising, or events)—at or in conjunction with male-only venues treated as tax-deductible business expenses

- Existence of requirements for mandatory arbitration of sex discrimination claims, including sexual harassment, as a condition of hiring or continued employment

Except for written company policies, most of this type of information is closely guarded by companies, but they do have it. They know who works for them at what salary rate, their gender, and their job classification. Reasons for non-disclosure usu-

> The arbitrators based their finding [of sex discrimination] on 28 hours of testimony about a statistical review of Merrill's hiring, promotion and pay practices . . . Merrill had only one district director, 11 regional vice presidents, and 5 sales managers who were women in a network of more than 15,000 brokers.
>
> Patrick McGeehan, "Panel Finds Bias Against Women at Merrill Lynch," *The New York Times*, 4/21/2004

ally invoke "competitive advantage." A more likely reason is that if women knew what they were being paid and how they are being promoted compared to men, they'd demand more money, quit, sue, or both. The numbers many companies would produce are likely to be pretty strong evidence of sex discrimination, and publishing them would open the way for lawsuits. (These would probably be the same firms that claim most sex discrimination actions are "frivolous." If the cases are indeed without merit and companies aren't discriminating, disclosure of pay and promotion statistics would help prove it.)

> [In agreeing to a $54 million sex discrimination settlement] Morgan Stanley, and all of Wall Street, scored an even bigger win: the statistics remain under wraps. No matter how generous a dollar settlement the commission garnered, it is still an important step short. Wall Street will make changes only when its culture, and the hard numbers of compensation and promotion, are exposed in open court. But don't hold your breath.
>
> Susan Antilla, "Money Talks, Women Don't," *The New York Times*, 7/21/2004

But there's a simple solution to that too. Companies can commit to internal audits for a few years, reported only to the board compensation committee. At the same time, they would institute goals for improvement and tie management pay, retention, and promotion to meeting those goals. With this kind of frontline accountability, it wouldn't take too long to get to a point where they could report their numbers openly, maybe even be proud of them. Ben & Jerry's has been doing this for years. In 2003 their social audit report (contained in the annual report) looked like this:

GENDER EQUITY

Category	Gender	Average Salary 2001	Average Salary 2002	Average Salary 2003
Manufacturing & Administration	female (100)	$25,976	$25,465	$29,507
	male (216)	$27,866 (.93-to-1)	$27,023 (.88-to-1)	$30,041 (.98-to-1)
Professionals	female (55)	$40,565	$45,851	$47,484
	male (62)	$39,095 (1.04-to-1)	$45,514 (1-to-1)	$46,738 (1.02-to-1)
Middle Managers	female (29)	$57,915	$75,461	$79,739
	male (29)	$59,068 (.98-to-1)	$75,985 (.99-to-1)	$80,425 (.99-to-1)
Senior Managers	female (2)	$90,297	$121,874	$132,151
	male (5)	$93,545 (.97-to-1)	$124,678 (.98-to-1)	$127,080 (1.04-to-1)

Ben & Jerry's Gender Equity Report

Unlike Ben & Jerry's, most companies jealously guard this kind of information. As mentioned previously, some even prohibit employees, on threat of firing, from discussing pay with coworkers. No wonder the pay gap persists. Making gender equity audits public ought to be viewed as a basic fairness tool. While companies can learn virtually everything about employees, from traffic tickets to health conditions, employees can learn almost nothing about employer behavior that affects them fundamentally. Knowing a company's record on hiring and promotion of women, pay relative to men, and whether management is held accountable for the outcomes women experience can make a real difference. Prospective employees could make a more informed decision about which job offer has the most promise. Current workers would have a realistic idea of their chances for advancement (or layoff) and whether those great slogans translate into action.

Gender equity audits could benefit companies as well. Management would be able to see at a glance what jobs women hold and how they're doing. If women aren't advancing as fast as men, it could be because they leave the company for another with more family-friendly policies. Or it could be the opposite—the policies are there, but men can "get ahead" by not taking advantage of them. So employers need to look at who is taking family leave, for how long, and what happens to them in the years following.

Companies with fifty or more employees are required by the Family and Medical Leave Act to grant twelve weeks of *unpaid* job-protected leave for workers caring for newborns, newly adopted children, or immediate family members with serious health conditions. Paid maternity leave is required only if the company gives paid leave for other disabilities, like heart attacks. (About 43 percent of women workers in the United States are entitled to some kind of paid maternity leave, most provided by state unemployment compensation systems. A measly 7 percent of employers offer paid paternity leave.[85])

Inducing men to take paternity leave and family leave, like shrinking the pay gap, would help change that family fairness balance as well as make women more competitive at work. But it is a real uphill challenge, and not just because in the United States mandated family leave is unpaid and most men would give up more money than their wives. The culture in most companies is that family and medical leave is a "woman's" benefit, even though the law is gender neutral and courts have ruled that men must be allowed to take it.

Much has been written about why men don't take advantage of family leave and how to increase their participation. Reasons vary from the obvious, which is that they can't afford it, to ingrained attitudes on the part of managers and even spouses. Married working mothers' attitudes about parenting are not often thought of as an obstacle to more men participating in caregiving, but there is no question that attitudes can be a barrier. Many mothers don't realize it, but they don't really want a full partner in child-raising. They want a helper who does it exactly as they dictate. They criticize the father if he messes up, sometimes redoing a task the father has already done. This has been dubbed "gatekeeping" by researchers. One large study of dual-earning couples with children found that approximately 20–25 percent of mothers engaged in some kind of gatekeeping behavior.[86] Without getting into a blame-the-victim mode here (because it's men's attitudes that traditionally have been far more resistant to child care), it's fair to ask: What difference does it make if the baby eats her bananas before her carrots or the booties don't match the blanket?

Strategies that have yielded higher "take up" rates for family leave by fathers in other countries have also been studied by researchers. High wage-replacement rates maximized the chances that fathers would take leave. Public education campaigns have reduced the cultural and institutional resistance to leave-taking by fathers as well. The Swedish government launched campaigns in the 1990s emphasizing the benefits of fathers taking parental leave to families, workplaces, children, and society. More than 40 percent of eligible Swedish fathers now take some leave in their child's first year—up from only 2 percent in 1974 when parental leave was introduced.[87]

Role modeling was a big part of the discussion in 2000 after Prime Minister Tony Blair decided to take family leave following the birth of his fourth child, and it apparently played a part in his decision. Cherie Blair urged her husband to follow the lead of the prime minister of Finland, who had taken paternity leave twice. He did. According to news reports: "This is a significant step in a direction it's not used to following: leaving tradition behind to act on a new federal policy that allows new dads to take up to 13 weeks' leave from their jobs." (Blair did not take the full thirteen weeks; he took a few days.[88])

Of course, even if men were convinced that family leave is the manly thing to do, they'd still have to be able to afford it. Most countries that allow men to take off have paid leave (though not 100 percent), either through a public subsidy or government-company partnership. And some countries have a "use it or lose it" model, where the family loses the man's share of paid leave if he doesn't take it. (The U.S. law actually produces that result too, but since our family leave is unpaid, a frequent outcome is that neither spouse can afford to take it.) A single state program (California) notwithstanding,[89] we're not likely to get government-administered paid leave in the United States. But companies (who don't want that government regulation anyway) are not prevented from providing some form of it themselves.

Ernst & Young, the global consulting firm with 23,000 U.S. employees scattered throughout ninety-five locations, instituted two weeks' leave at full pay (on top of the mandatory twelve weeks' unpaid leave under FMLA) in 2002. The company's workforce is roughly 50/50 women and men. In the first year, 46 percent of paid leave-takers were male. "We had taken an employee survey," said Maryella Gockel, director of Human Resources. "More paid time off was second in importance. Still, we were surprised and pleased that so many men took the leave the first year. It was used all the way up and down the line, from administrators to partners." How did the company convince men it was acceptable to take off? "We advertised it, and we encouraged it through regular communications, and we reminded people," she said. "And when the numbers came in, we advertised that too. It was all part of a family-friendly message. We made it seem 'normal' for men as well as women." It is probable that men in this company do not see taking the leave as threatening to their careers. The company values it enough to pay for it, advertises and encourages it, and 50 percent of their colleagues (women) are already more inclined to take advantage of it. It's doubtful, however, that as many men take advantage of the unpaid extension offered by FMLA, underscoring the importance of paid leave.

"Can't afford it," is the usual excuse for not providing paid leave. Some smaller companies probably would struggle, but the behemoth corporations usually find a way to pay for what they think is important. It's all a matter of priorities. In 2002, American Express settled a lawsuit for sex and age discrimination filed on behalf of more than four thousand women for $31 million.[90] If the company had not engaged in behavior resulting in this settlement on sex discrimination charges, and had that money available for paid family leave instead, it could have provided twelve weeks of leave for 2,583 employees at $1,000 per week. Even relatively smaller outlays could go a long way. If Citigroup cut the $63 million pay package of its Augusta National member chair Sanford

Weill by, say, $10 million a year, and eliminated another million in entertainment costs for wining and dining clients during Masters Tournament week, that could take care of leave for 1,833 employees at $500 a week.

Even if only some companies and not others instituted paid family leave, it would increase the overall number of men taking it. Unless both spouses worked for the same company, he'd be as likely as she to have an employer that paid. So if his company had the benefit and hers didn't, they could keep her full paycheck coming in while he stayed home with some partial compensation. If they were lucky enough to both work for a company that provided the benefit, a "use it or lose it" policy would probably guarantee that he took his share.

We've seen that another part of the systemic discrimination built into the corporate culture is the virtually unlimited hours that people on the upward track are expected to work. Again, we are talking about salaried workers who do not gain extra pay for staying extra time. What they do gain is the "dedicated" image—favor with the boss or a better or more extensive work product due to the extra hours they put in. Even though it cuts into the quality of their non-work lives, extra-time workers benefit at work. So companies need to change the culture—*mandate* a change in the culture—with formal limitations on work hours that are strictly enforced except in extraordinary circumstances.

"But we can't do it," we'll hear. "The workload is too high, we always have projects on deadline, and we can't just let our best thinkers pick up and go home just before the seven P.M. strategy session." Consider this: Before the 1980s—when work weeks started stretching above forty hours—somehow the cases all got argued, the insurance policies all got issued, the audits all got completed, the ads all got created, the stocks all got traded, the clients all got consulted, and the reports all got turned in.

Limiting hours is not a radical idea. It's not even a new idea; it's just no longer thought of as "normal." There is nothing stopping most companies from doing it, protestations notwithstanding. Suppose it did take a few more workers? Profits are at historic highs ($1 trillion in 2003, a recession year, and the highest ever recorded in U.S. history[91]), and new people could probably be hired from the savings in turnover alone. (The cost of turnover is about 1.5 times the salary of the average departing employee, and it goes up to about twice the salary for professionals.[92]) There is no question employee loyalty would skyrocket. If spreading the work among more people is impossible, it's still a good bet that the work would get done in the time available—it always has. Loyal, less-stressed employees are more productive.

The idea of mandatory limits on work hours is standard in Europe, and Europeans work less than their American counterparts. Conversely, the United States has no limit on hours a person can be required to work, except for some very narrow exceptions affecting public safety—health workers and truck drivers. Eighty-six percent of full-time employees work forty hours or more.[93] When the forty-hour work week as the threshold for overtime pay was first introduced through the Fair Labor Standards Act in 1938, it was done partially to increase employment by spreading the available work to more individuals.[94] The idea that limiting the work week would have the added benefit of allowing more people to be employed was also partially behind the most recent work hour reduction instituted in France in 2000.

The argument can be made that limiting hours is not necessary—what we need is flextime, telecommuting, and compressed work weeks. Under these arrangements there are usually core hours when people must be on the job, with flexibility at other times as long as the work gets done. Most such arrangements dictate a *minimum* number of hours (usually forty) but do not limit the *maximum* number of hours. There is no question that flexibility could help with juggling family demands, just as part-time and job sharing can. But as long as one group of employees (usually men) is free to ignore these options and put in extra hours and face time with the boss, those who take advantage of them (usually women) are likely to fall behind in pay and advancement opportunities. And the reality is that only a fraction of U.S. companies have even one of these arrangements, much less the full range of options. It would be much more straightforward to simply limit work hours and enforce the limit except under very narrow circumstances. If everyone, including managers, was subject to the limit, there would be no one there for the extra-hours worker to impress. (Yes, there would be exceptional times where deadlines could not be avoided, but they should be treated as truly exceptional and not be allowed to become the norm.)

Consider Young & Thompson, a boutique law firm near Washington, D.C. It employs twelve attorneys and fifty people overall. The usual hours are 10:30 to 6:30. How do they do it? "The partners set the standard," says one new hire. "And we manage the work. People do not work holidays or weekends. When you know these are the work hours, you get the work done. We may make slightly less than we could at some other firms, but everybody is happier. It's not worth the 10 percent more money we might get elsewhere."

It is true that limiting work hours takes money directly from hourly workers, so some would argue that mandating shorter work weeks would hit hourly workers much harder than others. It would, if wages are not high enough to make it on shorter hours. But in reality, companies routinely limit hourly workers to just under the minimum needed to automatically gain benefits (thirty-five hours per week in 2004), forcing them to work two separate low-wage, no-benefit jobs to make ends meet.

Even with family-friendly policies and reasonable work hours, juggling to find child care and worrying about kids while at work is a sap on employee productivity—again falling more on women than men. Most working parents cobble together some kind of child care—they have to. How to provide better care has been an ongoing debate in Congress and among advocates for several decades, and many full-sized volumes on the topic can be found. Corporate America alone cannot solve the child care problem in the United States, and the government is not going to do it so long as voters don't view it as a public responsibility. But some workplaces have more enlightened polices than others, and more companies following their example could go a long way in achieving gender parity at work. The spouse with on-site child care or company-assisted arrangements near the workplace is more likely to take responsibility for getting the kids dropped off every day. That could as easily be the father as the mother. Even if on-site child care is not available, other assists like emergency care and child care vouchers for times when regular caregivers are unexpectedly unavailable could also help equalize the gender landscape. Many companies offer some version of this. Fannie Mae headquarters in Washington, D.C., offers on-site emergency child care and an emergency child care voucher program for up to twenty-five days at their other facilities. Does all this cost money? Of course. But think of it as "burden sharing," to borrow a phrase from the government. Child care costs parents a huge portion of their income now, while most employers get off without laying out a dime. Paying a fair share for employee well-being, not to mention contributing to the well-being of the future workforce, would seem to be just that: *fair.*

None of the solutions put forward here is a panacea for gender imbalances at home or at work. But all are systemic solutions to systemic forms of sex discrimination that are still built into the American workplace and keep power from expanding beyond its traditional base. And none of them is impossible. In fact, all are already being done with very positive results. But it takes more than lip service. It takes a true dedication to *outcomes,* not just ideals, and the willingness to spend resources to get there. Individuals will still need to compete, and individual expertise will still triumph, but the rules of engagement will be different. A gender lens—in this case seeing things from the female perspective—can help. And as we'll see in the next chapter, being a woman is not a requirement.

A Few Good Men

In the Augusta National controversy, there were many men in the press, in Congress, and in public opinion leadership who advocated opening the doors to women. Julian Bond, chair of the board of the NAACP, sent out a press release early in the conflict expressing the support of his organization, and making the explicit connection between race and gender discrimination. Sam Pryor, a New York attorney, gave critical help when NCWO needed resources to investigate the legal case. Martin Luther King III took a strong stand and provided people and resources for the news conference and demonstration in Georgia, as did Jesse Jackson of Rainbow/PUSH. Georgia Governor Sonny Perdue spoke out (Hootie publicly rebuked him with a "shut up" letter), and Senator Vincent Fort introduced a resolution against Augusta's policies in the Georgia legislature. New York City Council member Oliver Koppell spearheaded a strongly worded letter to CBS from the Council. Cary Goodman coordinated press events with New York City Council members and a demonstration in front of CBS. Tim Smith, senior vice president of Walden Asset Management, and Gary Brouse of the Interfaith Center on Corporate Responsibility led the effort by socially responsible investors to put pressure on both the New York Stock Exchange (interim CEO John Reed is a member) and the CEOs in the financial sector.* Cyrus Mehri and Steve Skalet continue to lend the resources of their law firm to investigate charges of sex discrimination at Augusta-related companies. Even comedian David Letterman did his part by continually poking fun at Hootie and the club members.

But save one individual, former CBS president Thomas Wyman,† who publicly resigned his Augusta National membership in disgust, *those who actually had the power to make change elected not to do it*. The sponsors could have done it. The golfers could have done it. The ruling bodies of golf could have done it, and most or all the CEO members could have done it. It wouldn't even have taken a majority. Imagine a dozen or so of the most powerful men in business standing together at a news conference declaring the exclusion of women unacceptable. Even the *threat* of such a thing would probably have changed the policy (the same is true for the golfers). But these guys are only willing to declare their support for women when there are no consequences and no accountability, like at those diversity award ceremonies or

---

*A letter was sent to John Reed and the eight CEOs of the financial sector who hold memberships in Augusta National (American Express, Bank of America, Citigroup, Prudential, JPMorgan Chase, Morgan Stanley, Berkshire-Hathaway, Franklin Templeton). The letter was signed by some forty firms and organizations representing socially responsible investors with billions of dollars under management. None of the CEOs replied or acknowledged the letter in any way.

†Wyman died a few weeks after his resignation, so the impact on the other members was minimal. Members widely viewed the only other resignation (John Snow, when he was nominated for Secretary of the Treasury) as one of expedience, not conviction, and some expect him to be invited back once his term is completed.

when they give money to foundations that encourage both boys and girls to take up sports like golf—a sport in which the girls can't participate as equals when they grow up.

"Sharing the power" is a phrase we hear often, and many of those giving lip service to advancing women in the workplace use it in official company jargon. On the surface it's not a bad goal, until you think about what the words actually mean. The word *sharing* itself connotes ownership. We're taught this from kindergarten. Your brother has an ice-cream cone but is willing to *share* it, or you have a box of crayons and the teacher tells you to *share* with the kid next to you. But the basic notion is that while someone who owns something might be willing to give you a bit of it, it's still *theirs*. Sharing the power with women is done all the time in the workplace—with a few select women who are not a threat so long as they *are* few and select.

Widening the power base beyond its traditional boundaries is a different concept entirely. It means extending the ownership of power to those who have been mostly or entirely left out. Only the present power holders can do this—mostly men. Until a critical mass is reached, the few women in positions to widen the power base are pretty much alone, or in a distinct minority, making them vulnerable to accusations of "special interest mentality" or, worse, "pushing a feminist agenda."

While it is obvious from the numbers alone that many men in power consider maintaining the male power base part of their job (some unconsciously), not all subscribe to this. Just as Bobby Kennedy had the social conscience to found the Federal City Club when African-American men were excluded from the other centers of informal power in Washington, some have led the way to end the exclusion of women in positions and places of power. In 1975, President Ford refused to attend Washington's famous Gridiron dinner—a powerfest between top government leaders and the press—unless women were admitted. Women have been attending ever since, and they are now an integral part of the Gridion Club's membership. President Jimmy Carter in 1977 added sex, religion, and national origin to the *Federal Personnel Manual*'s rule against official participation of federal employees in conferences and meetings held at racially exclusive facilities. Governor Hugh Carey of New York followed suit in 1980 for his state employees. Senator Ted Kennedy, while chair of the Senate Committee on the Judiciary, began to require that nominees for the federal bench resign from discriminatory clubs, leading the way for the U.S. Judicial Conference to adopt a code of conduct for all federal judges to withdraw from race and sex discriminatory clubs in 1981.

Government has always been ahead of business when it comes to ending discrimination against women in both formal and so-called "informal" settings, but men in the private sector have taken the lead as well. As early as 1977, Richard Salant, NBC's vice chairman, resigned from New York's Century Club over its refusal to admit women,[95] saying he was offered a job at a meeting there. "They claim that it's social, but there is business there." Vern Atwaters, chairman of the Board of New York City's Central Savings Bank, testified before the Senate Banking Committee in 1979 that significant business opportunities were denied women when they did not have the same access to the private clubs used by men to establish relationships and entertain prospective clients.

Ending discrimination against women in informal venues, like so-called "private" clubs where deals are made and relationships are solidified, must be done before women can truly compete on an equal basis with men at high levels in business. But ending discrimination against women in the workplace and society itself will benefit women up and down the line, from the first entry-level clerk to the executive suites. This is a much harder task than giving up a golf membership—it means changing the culture. A few men have been up to the challenge, and their leadership shows the way to widening the power base beyond its traditional boundaries.

Unlike the CEOs of major corporations who continue to deny sex discrimination even when it is documented, Massachusetts Institute of Technology president Robert Vest took immediate steps to remedy gender discrimination at his university when a damning report came out in 1999. He reviewed salary and promotion data, as well as resource allocation to female scientists. Instead of covering up or explaining away, he admitted the shortcomings and put in processes to correct the problems. His action was so novel it made national headlines.

Stewart Bainum was in the Maryland State House of Delegates from 1979–1983, where he was a member of the powerful Ways and Means Committee. He served in the Maryland Senate from 1983–1987, where he was a member of the Budget and Taxation Committee. After five years of failed legislative attempts to end tax breaks for private clubs that discriminate in Maryland, he urged his sister to file a discrimination suit against Burning Tree Country Club, where presidents have played golf in the past and a number of members of Congress still do. The Maryland Attorney General joined the suit. They won in Judge Irma Raker's court, but an appeals court created a loophole for the club. It took Bainum another year to get a bill passed to take tax breaks away from country clubs that discriminate in Maryland. (Burning Tree elected to give up their tax breaks—worth nearly a million dollars per year—instead of opening to women.)

Today Stewart Bainum is chairman of Choice Hotels International:

In the Burning Tree fight, I had some trouble with some of my legislative colleagues. The presiding officers named conferees who opposed the bill. They were more loyal to the old boy network than to what was right. I'm afraid many legislators will often just go along with the powers that be, rather than follow their consciences. Go along to advance their careers. Even years later some club members refuse to shake my hand when we are introduced at social events.

At Choice Hotels and our other businesses, diversity is one of our key standards of performance for our managers. It's a value which must permeate the organization, and infiltrate all of the systems and every process. We make it part of our evaluation of each of our leaders at every level of the organization. It is important to annually set goals and then *measure* how we do—that's fundamental. We're not where we want to be yet. It is somewhat of a journey, but we are making steady progress.

The CEO's primary responsibilities are threefold: creating a vision for the organization after listening to its employees and customers; recruiting extraordinary talent at every level of the organization; and managing the values of the organization. This means the CEO must walk the talk, including overcoming discrimination in the organization. Diversity goals must be integrated into all organizational processes and systems. It affects who you hire.

While it is a journey, it should not be an odyssey. If the steps are too small it is only lip service.

The problem with the board of directors is inbreeding. It is an incestuous process.

Creating a system where women and minorities can advance takes a lot of work. You must set goals. At Manor Care [where he was CEO] we spent eighteen to twenty days a year reviewing the top 2,500 managers in the organization and ranked them as to their performance and potential. We asked, "What actions must we take to recruit a sufficient number of talented women and minorities?" It was fun!

People planning is how you determine the capacity and integrity of an organization. The product of that annual people-planning process was a set of goals for the number of talented women and minorities we wanted to recruit and promote over each of the next three to five years at the various levels of the organization. Over eight or nine years this process helped change the culture of the company for the better.

There is no silver bullet for changing the culture of a corporation. A lot of different actions and tactics are required, which must emanate from the organization's values. These values must be consistently articulated through organizational behavior *at each level*. The key is to push people to take these goals seriously. And when a manager's record of performance to these goals directly affects their compensation and personnel evaluations, they do take them seriously. It is necessary to move aside people who do not want to live out these values. It has to be a change in culture, and you can't get there with non-cooperators.

The old boy network is very strong. It is difficult to

comprehend the exclusionary mindset of the Augusta members. You would think that they would want to send an inclusive signal to their employees. But they seem to have somewhat of a middle school mentality.

The guy at the top must set the standard.

Howell Raines was executive editor at *The New York Times* during the height of the Augusta National controversy. From the beginning, Raines saw the story as one about society and sex discrimination, not sports. The paper gave the story front page coverage at times and editorialized against the all-male policy. (This was not new for the *Times*—it had editorialized against all-male clubs two decades earlier, when women in New York were trying to gain entrance to enclaves like the University Club, where business was done routinely.) Two opinion columns that did not agree with the paper's editorial position on Augusta National were "spiked," causing a separate media firestorm and controversy over the coverage (the columns later ran). Not everyone at the paper agreed with Raines as to the importance of the Augusta fight, and when he was pushed out due to unrelated circumstances surrounding Jayson Blair, a reporter who had fabricated material, some tried to say his stand on the club was a contributing factor.

Many assumed my interest in the Augusta issue was because I was from the South and was involved in covering the civil rights movement, and that I was drawn by the parallels. That is not what governed the approach. *The New York Times* has always covered social issues as news. I have always been aggressively curious about how our society works, and the *Times* has a long history of fronting what Max Frankel called sociological stories. [The Augusta controversy] involved money, discrimination, media coverage, sports—all issues in our general society.

You didn't need to know much to know this was an important story about corporate America—important as something to watch for what it could tell us about the changed environment in corporate America in regard to shareholder opinion at a time when shareholders come from every sector of society, not just Wall Street. Can a corporation afford to do this—hold the executive memberships in a club that discriminates against women. If you are a CEO of a publicly held company and have shareholders of all genders, races, and stripes of political opinion, can your executives maintain a privacy barrier around those corporate memberships?

I was struck by the degree to which CBS was powerless. For decades it was the iconic network coverage in regard to social fairness. They were aggressive on migrant workers and civil rights and I was sensitive to the implications of that. I thought the story on CBS [their refusal to drop the Masters broadcast] should be looked at for what it told us about changes in broadcasting—how CBS now lacked the economic independence to stand up to a sponsoring organization and call the shots on what events the network would broadcast.

I knew this was a legitimate running news story as a business story, as a media story, and as a sociological story. In the larger society, even in the South and other conservative areas, I sense a higher sensitivity to women in the workplace. I don't sense a general decline in interest in equality for women. Conservative politicians have been very effective in creating a sense of oppression among the most privileged. They have declared discussion of sex discrimination unfashionable. They have a current lack of interest in civil rights. But as journalists we can't let that blind us to the fact that Augusta National has been a focus of discrimination issues since the Eisenhower administration.

I do not recall a gender difference in reaction within the *New York Times* staff as to how the Augusta story was covered. Certainly Selena Roberts and Dave Anderson were poles apart in what they wrote. I would have expected the feminists to attack Dave, but that wasn't the case. Nor did Selena's very tough columns about Hootie and the Augusta ethos cause internal controversy. At the time, there was a broader anxiety about changes at the paper as we moved toward broader definitions of news and more incisive reporting and analysis. Some regarded our aggressive coverage of a sports story as somehow "un-*Times*ian" since Augusta was a private club. On these questions, there's always an interaction between editors and reporters. But when a reporter gets the critical exclusive interview with Tiger Woods, given Augusta's history of discriminating against black golfers, I felt the story needed attention. It's something you have an obligation to share with your readers. At that time, too, we were trying to break the artificial wall between sports coverage and "real" news. Sports is so important in our society as a matter of economics and role models, it has to be looked at in a more journalistically challenging way. It's no longer a matter of just recording the scores. There are many facets to sports, including the ongoing stories of drugs and gender discrimination, that all have to be covered.

Gender fairness in hiring and promotion is a fact of constant awareness at the paper. We required managers to put matters of national origin, sexual preference, gender, and religion on the same basis as race. Multifaceted diversity was the goal. Leadership on gender at the paper has been easy because the publisher is comfortable with being a progressive example. Putting rhetoric into operation could be frustrating. One of the things to look out for when you are the top—do you have a pool of properly and equitably prepared people from which you can promote? That means giving everyone access to the experiences that will allow them to develop their full potential and move up.

As editor of the editorial page I created an editorial board of five out of ten writers being women. The top four editors were men, but never before had we had an editorial board where half the writers were women. There was a disparate number of lower salaries for women and minorities when I came on as editorial page editor. We started the process of building a board that reflected our diverse society and of aggressively breaking down these traditional compensation patterns. Changing those demographics was a prerequisite to progress. I wanted to root out traditional areas of discrimination. For example, we put in a general practice of reviewing salaries yearly, with an eye toward equal rewards based on merit, rather than simply following the patterns of the past.

In the newsroom, which is managed separately, we were lagging. Editors and managers had to be responsible for an ongoing diversity effort. The reality was uneven. The masthead has once again become heavily male. There is an organizational temptation to choose one small group and advance them through various work experiences and not pay enough attention to the pool. The hard part is building a large talent pool from which you draw. It needs constant attention. The good old boy network may not be in place anymore, but it still can affect the pipeline.

You don't have to fix things in a day. You can change the "gestalt" over time. I do not regret the amount of news coverage [on Augusta]. On the separate question of how you use the influence of the editorial page, when you want to change opinion you have to come at an issue again and again. I think that's what my successor as editorial page editor, Gail Collins, did as a matter of her independent judgment. In keeping with *Times* policy, there was no coordination between the news coverage and editorial comment.

Howard Dean served as governor of Vermont for eleven and a half years, from August 1991 to January 2003. Under Dean's leadership, more women were appointed to the judiciary and to senior government positions in Vermont than at any time in the state's history. Dean was thrust into the governorship when Governor Richard Snelling (R) died suddenly in August 1991. He was subsequently elected to five two-year terms. Dean campaigned for the Democratic nomination for President of the United States in 2003–2004. His training is as a medical doctor; before he entered public life he ran an internal medicine practice with his wife, who is still a full-time practicing physician.

I appointed more senior women than any other governor of Vermont. I appointed a chief of staff with experience.

She does the hiring—women get a better chance under women. It wasn't hard to do. When I became governor, I was already committed to feminist ideals, to equality under the law with equality of opportunity. I had a good team; I did not automatically assume that men were better.

I firmly believe in affirmative action. Not a quota, but we must assure a pool. Fifty percent of my judicial appointments were women. We did not have a quota, but we expanded the pool beyond the usual pool. Women and young people don't think of themselves as qualified. [More often than men] they think more qualifications are needed. We had a lot of quality. There were well-qualified women and men who didn't get through. But we put them up there in the pool. We reached out. There was no public backlash to our appointment of women. None. There was enormous discussion on gay rights, but women were not so controversial.

On down the line, we put diversity where it matters, in key hiring decisions. My chief of staff had worked for a very successful woman governor, Madeleine Kunin. They were effective, and they did keep an eye on pay equity. The wage structures [when I came in] did not reflect comparable work [for different job titles]. We reclassified some workforce titles that had been seen as traditionally female positions. We raised Cain with the state police to hire more women. There really were problems in harassment. We had to recruit because society has prejudices. It was hard—we really worked hard.

I often told the story on the campaign trail about asking if we could fill a policy analyst position with a man, because we had so many women in the department. And my chief of staff looked at me, and she wasn't thinking about what she was saying, and she said, "You're absolutely right there's a gender imbalance in the office, but it's really hard to find a qualified man." And I tell that story for a reason. It's not just fifty-five-year-old white guys like me; everybody tends to hire people like themselves. And since the preponderance of people who do the hiring in this country are guys like me, that's why you have to have affirmative action.

It's not because we're sexist and racist, it's because there's an unconscious bias in every human being to hire people like themselves. That is why women have lower pay rates than men, because they don't have the same ability to get the same jobs, even though they're qualified. We had to work to overcome the bias of the screening committee, which would tend to screen out women because the majority of the people on the screening committee were men.

Because we did hire a staff that looked like the rest of Vermont, we got some remarks from some of the old codgers: "There goes Dr. Dean and his nurses," and stuff like that. But they got used to it.

Al Neuharth is a lifelong journalist and entrepreneur who served as a groundbreaking CEO of the Gannett company in the 1970s. He founded the nation's largest-selling daily newspaper, *USA Today*, in 1982, with diversity policies that were unheard of in the newspaper industry. Neuharth was named the most influential person in print media for the 1980s by *Washington Journalism Review* (now *American Journalism Review*). He still writes a weekly column for the domestic and international editions of *USA Today* called "Plain Talk," which also appears in other newspapers nationwide. He was the first male from the newspaper industry to win Women in Communications' highest honor, the Headliner Award.

> In the workplace, particularly if you are selling a broad-based consumer product, the people who produce that product must be as diverse as the audience you are seeking. At *USA Today,* we established a policy that said the leadership must be as diverse as the readership. Goals were to reach all segments of society. Middle-aged white males can't develop those products and make the right decisions. They have blinders on.
>
> We edited somewhat by formula. Page 1 every day had to have X number of pictures that were nonwhites and non-males [others have said there had to be a minority and a woman above the fold]. Page 1 stories had to have broad appeal: politics, government, sports, health. Media has been criticized, generally fairly, to have run only negative news of minorities and sometimes women, and only positive news of good ole boy white males. We made it clear that stereotypes would not work. The pictures and stories had to match a variety of newsmakers. Editors couldn't allow black males to always be featured because they were criminals and live up to the policy.
>
> We tied management reviews and compensation to diversity in the newsroom and performance in the newsroom. Madelyn Jennings was head of HR at Gannett, and her number-one assistant was a black former football player, Jimmy Johnson. We sent them around the country to explain the policy to the middle-aged white males. It was easier with a new rather than an old institution,

though *USA Today* had some missteps. But our first managing editor for news was a woman.

USA Today was a new product and staff, so reminders were constant. At Gannett, some resisted the management reviews, and some of the spouses did as well. We always invited spouses to the general meetings and to the discussion afterward. Most of the spouses were females, but we had a few males. At one of our medium-sized papers, after we explained the policy, a female spouse of a white male stood up and said, "But who's going to look after my *husband's* interests?" I replied, "His interests have been more than taken care of for a long time."

We included spouses because we felt at Gannett prior to *USA Today* that most news workers are on the job twenty-four hours a day, no matter where they are. Having spouses and families made a better family performance; an all-consuming effort and they understood the commitment. Rosalynn Carter came on our board after the White House years. Jimmy Carter was our most prominent spouse, and he enjoyed it.

Our first managing editor for news was Nancy Woodhull. Her daughter Tennie was only three years old. Nancy worked long and late and she came to me and said, "There's a problem—not just for me but a number of others. I'm not home to put her to bed or read to her, so we need a place she can come—a family room where we can take time and have dinner and just visit." So we installed that. It caught on at other sites. And the incentive came from Nancy. A male with a stay-at-home wife would never have seen the need for it.

You can't insure your legacy. You have to make sure

the good guys and good girls outnumber the bad when you leave. It starts at the top, but it has to be enforced and continued down the line. So many good people have to be in key places.

USA Today is stronger now than it was then. We recently lost Karen Jurgensen, who got caught up in the [Jack Kelley, a reporter caught fabricating stories] scandal. I wrote a column saying she is taking a fall for a male-made mess. But she was at the top, and if women and men are going to be treated equally, it includes penalties. You can't have it both ways.

Vigilance is not a strong enough word for how you keep a policy like this in place and working. You have to be mean and tough when necessary. At *USA Today* we had an entirely new staff, and we had clear and rigid rules from the beginning. You couldn't be in management unless you subscribed to the rules. At Gannett we had eighty-plus papers, the majority run by white males, so it took longer.

We finally were successful because even middle-aged white males thought about their paychecks. We charted comparative pay and promotion in every way—including gender, race, and age of new hires. We looked at it every year. It had to be monitored and enforced. My favorite phrase to a manager that didn't meet the goals was, "Do you want to quit, get fired, or start over?" We had concrete goals for the next year, always. You have to have a measuring stick. You value what you measure.

These men have shown us through words and deeds that leadership from the top affects change all the way to the bottom rung. As important as their methods and ideas are for women, the model they provide for other men can ultimately make the most change. When a CEO takes action, good or bad, it legitimizes that action to the rest of society. Unlike the guys in the green jackets whose validation derives from being just like the others, not rocking the boat, not speaking out, and perpetuating discrimination, real men take the lead. Unfortunately, for every Al Neuharth there are still dozens of Philip Purcells, whose male executives entertain clients at strip clubs. For every Stewart Bainum there are hundreds, like Sanford Weill of Citigroup, who ignore their pay inequities and glass ceilings until the courts intervene, then drag the women who win a settlement through years of hassle before they pay off. For every Howard Dean, there are still legions of Jeffrey Immelts, who spend time and money on the appearance of fairness to women while continuing the same old practices that keep the number of females at the top miniscule. Changing the gender mix at the top can make a profound difference.

Women in High Places:
Why a Gender Lens Matters

There's an old saying in the women's movement that you can't become something until you can imagine it. Part of our job is getting people, especially girls, to imagine it. No, it doesn't mean becoming something that's impossible, like a world-class Quidditch player in a Harry Potter book, but that's actually not a bad parallel. It means doing something you couldn't have imagined yourself doing because you had never seen anyone like yourself doing it. Kids couldn't imagine being Quidditch players until J. K. Rowling allowed them to envision themselves doing it. In the old days (pre-1972) girls couldn't see themselves being professional soccer players or basketball players because no one had allowed them to imagine it. There were no role models, much less role teams, until Title IX made them possible. Girls were not only systematically kept out of sports, but many other places as well, like medical schools and law schools, so they couldn't see themselves becoming doctors or lawyers either. Without real-life examples, the idea of a woman doctor was hard for anyone to envision, especially young girls choosing their life's path. A common riddle at the time went like this:

A father and son are injured in a car accident, and in the confusion they are taken to separate hospitals. The son is taken to the emergency room immediately, and the surgeon looks at him and cries, "Oh my God, that's my son." How is this possible?

People just couldn't solve this riddle. They offered answers like, "The son was so badly injured the doctor mistook his identity," or "He wasn't the real son of the man injured in the wreck, he was his nephew." The simple answer—that the surgeon was the boy's mother, not his father—just wasn't in the realm of imagination for most individuals, male or female.

Today, of course, the riddle is easier, since we can all at least imagine women in just about any role, even if we haven't actually seen any women fulfilling those roles yet. President of the United States, of course, comes to mind, but there are plenty of others: Majority Leader of the Senate, Speaker of the House, Chairman of the Joint Chiefs of Staff, Secretary of Defense, Secretary of the Treasury, Vice President of the United States, President of the AFL-CIO, President of the American Medical Association or the American Bar Association or the U.S. Chamber of Commerce or the Business Roundtable, and CEO of 492 of the 500 largest corporations in America.

When it comes to viewing the world, the way you see things is shaped by many factors: race, class, marital status, age, religion, geography—and gender. Being able even to notice certain things, or see them in a way that's out of the ordinary for others looking at the same situation, by definition requires a different point of view. At any given time, we can think of viewpoint as one of those pairs of sunglasses with several colors of lenses that can be popped in and out for use on different days; each one highlights or filters out a certain portion of the available light spectrum.

Filters allow us to view the world from a certain point of view—and to see things (or not see them) in a different way from people wearing other lenses. Being able to imagine women in unexpected places—and to see their absence as odd and not "normal"—requires a different way of looking at the world than most of us have been taught. The gender lens is always available; most of us use it much of the time. One example I often use the gender lens on is the issue of gun control. When men think about guns they think about hunting, warfare, or even fantasize about being called to help the sheriff clean up Dodge. Women think about getting raped at gunpoint. Basic difference.

Christine Brennan highlighted this in that 2002 *USA Today* column when she pointed out the fact that sex discrimination at Augusta had been blatant for years, but everyone just took it for granted; there was *acceptable* (to men) and *unacceptable* (to men) discrimination. It wasn't, of course, acceptable to Brennan, nor to the woman who inspired her with the original article in *Golf for Women* about Augusta's blatant sexism, Marcia Chambers.

While men like Lloyd Ward were failing to notice the barring of women from Augusta National as both an example of and a metaphor for the exclusion of women in the halls of power, plenty of women in high places did notice. We heard from many anonymously, because they feared for their jobs. But like Brennan and Chambers, there were other women who could use their positions to call attention to the wrong that was Augusta, and to try to use their influence to make change.

"I am so mad about this situation," Helen Thomas told me.

"It reminds me of the girls in the balcony [when women were officially and militantly barred from the National Press Club]." In case Thomas's name doesn't ring a bell, she is the dean of the White House press corps, the person who for forty years asked the first question at formal news conferences, and said, "Thank you, Mr. President," at the end. I had talked to Thomas at a briefing at the National Press Club, where we were both serving on a panel about pay equity. "Send me some material on this," she continued. "I want to keep up with what is happening." I returned to the office and faxed background and comments, and some selected news stories.

When a few weeks later President Bush named John Snow, CEO of CSX Corporation, to become Secretary of the Treasury, the nomination was generally seen as appropriate. He was a Ph.D. in economics, a former deputy undersecretary for transportation, a college professor,

Until 1971, the National Press Club did not admit women as members. Female reporters (even Pulitzer Prize winners) were relegated to the balcony to cover the luncheon speeches and briefings by newsmakers, while male reporters (even the newest recruits) sat in the ballroom lunching with the powerful. There were no chairs in the balcony, no food or drink, and the women had to share the space with cameras, equipment, and technicians.

"It was so hot, it was so hot in that balcony. All those bodies jammed under the eaves. It was hard to hear, it was hard to see . . . All this standing—it was like a cattle car . . . We could not ask questions of the speakers . . . You entered and left through a back door, and you'd be glowered at as you went through the club quarters. It was discrimination at its rawest."

Nan Robertson, *The Girls in the Balcony* (New York: Fawcett, 1992)

and head of a major rail company. The nomination was completely unremarkable, except for one thing: Snow was a member of Augusta National. Thomas was probably the only reporter in the White House briefing room who even *remembered* that notorious Press Club balcony, much less had been consigned to it. So she noticed that an individual who apparently saw nothing wrong with sex discrimination was about to be elevated to the Cabinet. In the opening questions to the news briefing announcing the nomination, she asked about the membership. Several other questions followed. Despite some lukewarm denials from White House spokesman Ari Fleischer that it was "not a disqualifying factor" for a Cabinet position, Snow resigned his Augusta membership a few hours later.

One week later, *The Washington Post* reported that Oklahoma Senator Don Nickles, who was looking to replace Senator Trent Lott as the Senate's GOP leader, would not get the job because of his membership in the men-only Burning Tree Club, and that the club was "now off limits" to Bush Administration officials.

Had the press corps been all male, it is highly unlikely that anyone would have seen Snow's membership as an issue at all, much less important enough to potentially scuttle his confirmation. Thomas saw the nomination through the lens of her gender, and it was different from the male lens. It is doubtful that any future candidates for the Cabinet or other high-ranking positions will not be asked about membership in clubs that discriminate against women, just as they have been asked for a long time about race discriminatory memberships. A disqualifying factor indeed.

Other powerful women took up the cause. Again, the gender lens mattered. Remember that Amo Houghton, Republican

Congressman from New York, not only refused to resign his membership when exposed publicly, he declined even to say he supported opening Augusta National to women.[96] His female colleagues in the House viewed it differently. Led by Carolyn Maloney (D-NY), a resolution was introduced expressing the sense of Congress that elected government officials and political appointees are ethically bound not to belong to discriminatory clubs, even if such membership is nominally legal. Representative Louise Slaughter (D-NY) also publicly opposed Houghton on the issue, and she wrote a letter to *The New York Times* thanking reporter George Vecsey for his courage in writing a piece entitled "We Could Use More Martha Burks" immediately after the 2003 tournament and protest in Augusta.

Maloney's taking leadership on the resolution, cosponsored by John Lewis (D-GA) and several other House members both male and female, may have had an influence on other men taking up the cause in other contexts. Representative Brad Sherman (D-CA) joined Maloney in sponsoring a bill to outlaw the tax deductions companies enjoy for entertaining at clubs that discriminate. Senator Patrick Leahy prepared an amendment to a judicial pay raise bill that would have tied proposed raises to strengthened prohibitions against federal judges' belonging to discriminatory clubs.[97] There is no question that the Augusta National controversy heightened awareness of the gender power equation when George W. Bush signed the first federal abortion ban since *Roe v. Wade*. In a front-page photo that ran in newspapers across the country, Bush was shown flanked by an admiring chorus of smiling white men as he signed the bill, an image emblematic of male control over women, one that prompted Senator Frank R. Lautenberg (D-NJ) to say this on the Senate floor:

I rise to discuss something that struck me as downright chilling when I saw it yesterday. It was the signing of the so-called "Partial Birth" Abortion Bill. Here is a photo of the signing of this bill, which represents the most sweeping attack on women's rights in thirty years. What do we see? A group of gleeful men watching President Bush sign away women's rights. Look at this image again. There are no women on the stage. It's all men. It's downright frightening. **It looks like a board meeting of Augusta National—** not the signing of legislation to change the rights of women . . . These men are eager to snatch the rights away from women. The lack of women on this stage says: Make no mistake—we men are in charge. I have called it a "male-a-garchy." And this photo captures the essence of the male-a-garchy that women live under today.

When a congressional oversight committee held hearings on the United States Olympic Committee in early 2003, NCWO wrote to committee members calling for Lloyd Ward's resignation from the club (we later wrote committee members calling for his resignation from the USOC, which came about a month later). We pointed out that while he claimed to be working from the inside to change the policies at Augusta National, there was no evidence that he had done so, and the club had recently hardened its position—now they were saying they would *never* admit a woman. Both USOC president Marty Mankamyer and Senator Barbara Boxer (D-CA) were offended by Ward's membership in Augusta. So was Senator Ben Nighthorse Campbell, an ex-Olympian who was also on the committee that grilled Ward on ethics charges. But Mankamyer and Boxer explicitly objected to the membership because of the statement it made about women, while Nighthorse Campbell may have been more concerned about the image and integrity of the USOC overall. Certainly that was the view of Senator John McCain, whose staff told NCWO he "agreed with us in principle" that Ward's Augusta membership was wrong, but he would not make an issue of it during the hearings (Nighthorse Campbell did). Boxer went even further, specifically soliciting input from NCWO and telling Ward he should "respect not only female athletes but females in general." She put these questions to him:

- What specific efforts have you made toward the goal of eliminating gender discrimination at Augusta? What have been the concrete results?
- Do you plan to resign from Augusta National Golf Club if the club does not open its doors to women?
- What is your timetable for resignation from the Augusta National Golf Club if your efforts to break down the gender barrier are unsuccessful?

These examples of the gender lens at work demonstrate that the way women look at things can lead to decisions that are different and encompass a wider worldview. There are many others, far out of the context of private clubs, dealing with the exclusion of women in domestic and world affairs, and in business and commerce. Madeleine Albright, the first female Secretary of State (appointed in 1996 by President Clinton), elevated the importance of women's issues, and she instructed U.S. diplomats around the world to make the furtherance of women's rights a central priority of American foreign policy.[98] She reportedly routinely confronted leaders of Arab countries about the absence of women in their governments. She did not go to Jordan for King Hussein's funeral, citing the Arab Muslim practice of barring women from burial rites as the reason. She confronted Senator Jesse Helms, a vigorous opponent of the international women's human rights treaty, on his opposition. It would not have been impossible for a male Secretary of State to have done any of these things, but he would have had to adopt the female gender lens. While as we've seen, some men can and do accomplish this to widen the circle of power, no Secretary of State had done it in the 206 years prior to Albright's appointment.

Up until 1993, the National Institutes of Health (NIH) specifically excluded women from large research studies, even on predominantly female diseases like breast cancer. Congress never questioned it until a critical mass of women swept into office in 1992—the "year of the woman," when the number of female legislators doubled (to 10 percent). Viewing the NIH decision-making process through the gender lens, and not through the "convenience" lens that the agency had been using, the women set out to change the system, and did so. They used their power and numbers to create the Office of Research on Women's Health at NIH and to mandate the inclusion of women and minorities in clinical trials.[99]

Women in power can also prevent things from happening because they use a gender lens to set priorities that men may not attend to. There are gender gaps in the way women vote and in the bills they introduce in Congress, reflecting different priorities, regardless of party. Women prevented the assault weapons ban from going down in defeat—if they had voted against the ban in the same proportion as men, it would have failed by thirty votes. Similar gender gaps have been found in votes on Family and Medical Leave and the Brady gun control bill. While men still introduce the majority of bills deemed important to women and families, women propose a disproportionate share given their relatively small minority in Congress.[100]

Despite their low numbers, powerful women in business can and do take the lead in making change. Barbara Krumsiek, CEO of Calvert, the nation's largest family of socially responsible mutual funds, launched the Calvert Women's Principles in 2004. Going far beyond the notion of "diversity" that companies can so easily exploit, the principles are a comprehensive code of corporate conduct on gender equality. The Women's Principles are the first to focus *exclusively* on empowering, advancing, and investing in women around the globe. Krumsiek's view is wider than the male-oriented bottom-line approach most of her counterparts take. She knows (and pays attention to) the fact that female labor is the labor that is most often exploited in a gobalized marketplace. In exercising leadership in this area, she not only uses a gender lens, she is helping to shine a gender spotlight on corporate practices worldwide.

Lifetime Television celebrated its twentieth year in 2004. The network had two male presidents before Carole Black took the helm in 1999. Her predecessors had dabbled in advocacy, but when Black took over as president and CEO, it became the DNA of the brand.

Before Black, manager Meredith Wagner had developed campaigns on breast cancer, child care, and the women's vote, and proposed a number of others. But Wagner never had the full muscle of the company behind her. When Black came to Lifetime, she gave Wagner, by now a top executive, the resources to take advocacy to the next level. She hired a female policy team in Washington to ensure that the programming was authoritative on issues, and to launch a key initiative—Stop Violence Against Women. It includes lobbying on legislation such as the Violence Against Women Act, and a week of high-profile events in Washington each year so lawmakers don't forget that one in three women faces violence at some point in her life.

Black insists that all departments at the company—not just Public Affairs—get behind the advocacy. Telephone numbers and websites where viewers can find help on any serious topic touched on now appear at the end of much of the programming. Black created this "tagging project"—even though it takes promotional and advertising time that could be sold—because she wanted the company to focus on *supporting women* on the issues that matter to them and their families. And though she knows no company is perfect, Black tries to evaluate every Lifetime corporate partnership in light of how that partner company treats women.

No doubt because of the gender lens, Black has made sure that programming at Lifetime Television for Women isn't just about the bottom line, but about the lives of its female viewers. Is it any surprise that she took the network from sixth to number one?

The examples here show us that individual women (and groups of women that have reached a critical mass) can influence both policy and outcomes. But we've also seen that it is still necessary to have the support of men, who ultimately hold the power. In Congress, men still hold 87 percent of the seats, so their endorsement is crucial to advancing women's priorities. In business, the CEO power, the board power, and the management power is still overwhelmingly male. So widening the circle beyond its traditional base clearly requires those who hold that power to have the courage to put aside a strictly male gender lens and look at the world another way.

When a prevailing culture does harm, and its traditions become contrary to the values of society at large, then it must change. When women were not allowed to enter colleges and universities and racial minorities were barred from restaurants and hotels, these standards were both created and enforced by the dominant white and male cultures. Slowly people (including those in power, with a hefty push from those out of power) realized that some manifestations of cultural values were harming whole groups, so societal standards changed. And the cultures changed, at least publicly. With the possible exception of some enclaves in Georgia, you will find that there are virtually no men today who believe women shouldn't have access to higher education, and only a very tiny minority of whites would still bar people of color from lunch counters.

Despite this, the argument continues about the proper place of women in society, whether we really should be co-owners of jobs, good pay, and equal opportunities, or whether we're "outsiders" who want to take something away from its rightful owners. When you own something you have power over it, most of all the power not to give it up or share it.

The general belief among insiders and outsiders alike is that Augusta National Golf Club will open to women—when Hootie Johnson is gone, or when enough time has passed that members can deny that NCWO brought it about. But even if Augusta National never admits women, the controversy will have served its purpose. It took us far beyond those hallowed gates and opened a national dialogue about fairness and the fact that gender bias is still all too often viewed as acceptable.

It also highlighted some very dark corners of discrimination that spill over into corporate attitudes and practices every day. We learned that even in the twenty-first century there are many Americans who believe women's place is second place (and more who don't), there are powerful men at the top who are dedicated to a world where gender bias is as unacceptable as race bias (and still too many who aren't), and there are systemic barriers to women in society and the workplace that no individual can overcome alone. But we've also seen that there are systemic solutions that most people of good will can endorse.

Whether the green jackets will ever be measured for the female body or not, sanctioning sex discrimination by those in power, even through so-called "benign" activities like golf, will be tainted with public disapproval. By resisting change so fiercely, perhaps Augusta National will have ultimately helped to hasten the day when the closed cult of corporate power is transformed into an open circle that includes everyone.

APPENDIX

AUGUSTA NATIONAL MEMBERS AND AFFILIATIONS*

A. T. Cross: Boss, Bradford, Retired
    Murray, J. Terrence, Director

Aaron Rents, Incorporated: Robinson, Ray, Director

Abbott Laboratories: Fuller, H. Laurance, Director

Accel-KKR: Hazen, Paul, Chairman

Accenture Energy Advisory Board: Shultz, George, Chairman

Acquavella Art Dealer: Acquavella, William, Principal

Acuity Brands, Incorporated: Robinson, Ray, Director

Adolph Coors Company: Coors, Peter, Chairman, Coors Brewing Company

Advantage Carolina Leadership Board: Dickson, Thomas, Former Chair

Aetna, Incorporated: Jordan, Michael, Director

Affymetrix, Incorporated: Loucks, Vernon, Director

Air Products & Chemicals, Incorporated: Murray, J. Terrence, Director

AK Steel Corporation: Fites, Donald, Director

Albany Law School: Anderson, Warren, Advisory Committee

Alcan Aluminum Ltd.: Culver, David, CEO, Retired

Alcoa, Incorporated: Hampel, Ronald, Director

Alester G. Furman: Furman, Alester, Retired

Alexis de Tocqueville Society: Boeschenstein, William, Donor

Alfred P. Sloan Foundation: Gilbert, S. Parker, Trustee

---

*The membership list is accurate for the period 2002–2004 so far as could be verified through published lists in *USA Today* and other sources, and miscellaneous press reports. Augusta National Golf Club has never confirmed or denied any name on the list.

All-American Wildcatters: Fluor, Peter, Member

Allegheny Conference on Community Development: Love, Howard, Member Emeritus

Allegiance Corporation: Knight, Lester, Chairman and CEO, Retired

Allied Bank of Georgia: Knox, Boone, Trustee

Allstate Corporation: Brennan, Edward, Director

ALLTEL Corporation: Townsend, Ronald, Director
Ford, Joe, Chairman
Ford, Scott, President, CEO, and Director
Stephens, Warren, Director

Alpha Partners: Hillman, Henry, Capital Provider

Alpine Group, Incorporated: Jansing, John, Director

Altria Group, Incorporated: Reed, John, Director

Ambase Corporation: Rice, W. Thomas, Former Director

Amerada Hess Corporation: Brady, Nicholas, Director

American Academy of Arts and Sciences: Reed, John, Treasurer
Bechtel, Riley, Fellow
Buffett, Warren, Member

American Bailey Corporation: Bailey, Ralph, Chairman and CEO

American Bar Foundation: Barrett, Hale, Fellow

American College of Healthcare Executives: O'Herron, Edward, Honorary Fellow

American College of Physicians: Battey, Louis, Fellow

American Cyanamid (now Wyeth/BASF): Affleck, James, Retired
Culver, David, Former Director

American Electric Power Company, Incorporated: Howell, William, Director

American Enterprise Institute: Raymond, Lee, Trustee and Vice Chairman
Galvin, Christopher, Trustee

American Express: Chenault, Kenneth, Chairman and CEO
Clark, Howard, Chairman, Retired
Robinson, James, Former CEO
McGinn, Richard, Director
Culver, David, Former Director
Williams, Joseph, Former Director
Laird, Melvin, Former Director, IDS Mutual Funds Group

American General Corporation: Davis, W. Lipscomb, Director

American Museum of Natural History: Shipley, Walter, Trustee

American Newspaper Publishers Association: Anderson, Harold, Former Head

American Petroleum Institute: Raymond, Lee, Chairman
Derr, Kenneth, Director
Fluor, Peter, Member

American Productivity and Quality Center: Derr, Kenneth, Director

American Society for Engineering Education: Galvin, Christopher, Member

American Standard, Incorporated: Marquard, William, Former President and CEO

American Stock Exchange: Moseley, Frederick, Governor

American Textile Machinery Exhibition-International: Chapman, Robert, Director

Amoco: Morrow, Richard: Chairman and CEO, Retired
  Beall, Donald, Former Director

AMR Corporation: Purcell, Philip, Director
  Brennan, Edward, Director

AmSouth Bancorporation: Nielsen, Claude, Director
  Ingram, David, Community Advisory Board

AMX Corporation: Winters, J. Otis, Director

Anadarko Petroleum Corporation: Butler, John, Director

Anderson Fund: Anderson, Wendell, President

Anheuser-Busch Companies, Incorporated: Warner, Douglas, Director
  Loucks, Vernon, Director
  Whitacre, Edward, Director
  Knight, Charles, Director
  Payne, William, Director

Aon Corporation: Knight, Lester, Chairman
  Perkins, Donald, Former Director

Applied Technology Investors, Incorporated: Moseley, Frederick, Former Director

Apriva, Incorporated: Robinson, James, Board Member

Aqua-Vac Systems: Taylor, F. Morgan, Chairman

Arcadia Partners: Stone, Robert, Director

ARCO International Oil & Gas: Bowlin, Mike, Retired

Argosy Gaming Company: Brennan, Edward, Director

Arkansas, State of: Ford, Joe, Former State Senator

Arkansas Best: Marquard, William, Chairman

Arnold Palmer Golf: Lupton, John, Position unavailable

Art Institute of Chicago: Bryan, John, Chairman of the Board of Trustees

ArvinMeritor: Poling, Harold, Director
  Beall, Donald, Former Director

ASI Holding Corporation: Marquard, William, Chairman Emeritus

Aster-Cephac SA: Culver, David, Former Director

AT&T: Dorman, David: Chairman and CEO
  Derr, Kenneth, Director
  Allen, Robert, CEO and Chairman, Retired
  Weill, Sanford, Former Director
  Perkins, Donald, Former Director
  Robinson, Ray, President, Southern Region
  Fites, Donald, Director, Wireless Services

Atlanta Arts Alliance: Yates, Charles, Retired

Atlanta Chamber of Commerce: Driver, Walter, Director

Atlanta Committee for the Olympic Games: Payne, William, President and CEO
    Chapman, Hugh, Chair, Finance Committee

Atlanta Junior Golf Association: Yates, Danny, Former Director

Atlantic Council of the United States: Hannan, Kenneth, Director

Atlantic Extrusions: Wearn, Wilson, Former Director

Atlantic Richfield Company: Bowlin, Mike, Former CEO and Chairman

Augusta Bar Association: Barrett, Hale, Member

Augusta Cab: Douglass, Edwin, President

Augusta Foundation: Boardman, Clayton, Director

Augusta National Golf Club/Masters Tournament: Stephens, Jackson, Former
Chairman

Augusta National, Incorporated: Johnson, William, Chairman

Augusta State University: Blanchard, Thomas, Business School Advisory Board
    Evans, Nick, Trustee

Augusta Tomorrow: Barrett, Hale, Chairman
    Boardman, Clayton, Director, Former President

Avnet, Incorporated: Robinson, Ray, Director

B. F. Goodrich: Houghton, Amory, Former Director

BAE Systems: Hampel, Ronald, Former Director

Balentine & Company: Ingram, David, Advisory Board Member

Baltimore Symphony Orchestra: Weill, Sanford, Director

Bank of America: Lewis, Kenneth, Chairman, President, and CEO
    Hance, James, Vice Chairman and CFO
    Townsend, Ronald, Director
    McColl, Hugh, Chairman and CEO, Retired
    Armacost, Samuel, Former President and CEO
    Chapman, Robert, Former Director
    Cousins, Thomas, Venture Business Associate
    Herlihy, Edward, Assisted Merger, NationsBank
    Lewis, David, Former Director, San Francisco
    Cooley, Richard, Chairman and CEO, Seafirst Bank, Retired

Bankers Information Technology Secretariat: Blanchard, James, Former Chair

Bankers Trust/Deutsche Bank: Herlihy, Edward, Assisted Merger

Bankrate, Incorporated: O'Block, Robert, Director

Bass Brothers Land, Incorporated: Anderson, Lyle, Business Associate

Bassett Furniture: Spilman, Robert, President and CEO

Baxter International, Incorporated: Knight, Lester, Former Vice President

Baxter Travenol Labs: Loucks, Vernon, Chairman and CEO, Retired

Bay Area Council: Biaggini, Benjamin, Former Chairman

Bayer AG: Reitzle, Wolfgang, Former Director

BCI Partners: Remey, Donald, Cofounder

Bechtel Group, Incorporated: Bechtel, Riley, Chairman and CEO
    Bechtel, Steve, Chairman Emeritus
    Gluck, Frederick, Former Vice Chairman and Director
    Haynes, Harold, Director
    Shultz, George, Director

BellSouth Corporation: Blanchard, James, Director

Belo Corporation: Moroney, James, Publisher and CEO
    Ward, Lloyd, Director

Berkshire Hathaway Incorporated: Buffett, Warren, Chairman and CEO

Berkshire Hills Bancorp: Bossidy, Lawrence, Director

Berman, Kalmbach & Company: Kalmbach, Dohn, Partner

Bessemer Trust Company: Phipps, Ogden, position unavailable
    Kirkland, David, Director

Beta Capital Group, LLC: Jordan, Michael, Partner

Bethlehem Steel Corporation: Foy, Lewis, CEO, Retired

Bill & Melinda Gates Foundation: Gates, William, Co-Chairman

Bio-Research Laboratories Ltd.: Culver, David, Former Director

Birmingham Budweiser Distributing Company Incorporated: Dobbs, John C., President

Birmingham Museum of Art: Blount, William, Finance Committee

Birmingham-Southern College: Blount, William, Trustee

Birmingham Steel: de Windt, E. Mandell, Former Director

Bissell Companies, Incorporated: Harris, John, Former President

Black & Decker Manufacturing Company: Peterson, Peter, Former Director

BlackRock, Incorporated: O'Brien, Thomas, Director

Blackstone Group: Peterson, Peter, Chairman
    Kennedy, Robert, Advisory Board

Blake Clark Enterprises: Clark, Blake, Principal

Blanchard & Calhoun: Blanchard, Thomas, President

Blount, Incorporated: Blount, William, Director

Boardman Petroleum: Boardman, Clayton, CEO

Boeing Company: Haynes, Harold, Former Director

Boston Stock Exchange: Moseley, Frederick, Governor

Boston Symphony Orchestra: O'Block, Robert, Chairman, Board of Overseers

Boy Scouts of America: Coors, Peter, Denver Area Council Executive Board
    Blount, William, Former Member, Executive Board

BP Amoco: Morrow, Richard, Retired
    Fuller, H. Laurance, Co-Chairman, Retired
    Knight, Charles, Director

Bradley Center Sports and Entertainment Corporation: Colbert, Virgis, Director

Brascan Corporation: Blanchard, James, Former Director

Brentwood Associates: Hillman, Henry, Capital Provider

Bristol-Meyers Squibb Company: Robinson, James, Director
  Gerstner, Louis, Director
  Allen, Robert, Director
  Adam, Ray, Director, Retired

British Petroleum: Ferris, Richard, Former Director

Brookings Institution: Daniel, D. Ronald, Honorary Trustee
  Robinson, James, Trustee

Bundy: Anderson, Wendell, Retired

Burlington Northern Santa Fe Corporation: Whitacre, Edward, Director

Burson-Marsteller: Seaman, Irving, position unavailable

Business Council: Welch, John, Former Chairman
  Garvin, Clifton, Former Chairman
  Jones, Reginald, Former Chairman
  Bechtel, Riley, Member
  Budd, Edward, Member
  Derr, Kenneth, Graduate Member
  Fites, Donald, Graduate Member
  Galvin, Christopher, Graduate Member
  Harrison, William, Member
  Houghton, James, Member
  Jordan, Michael, Member
  Love, Howard, Member
  Mettler, Ruben, Member
  Opel, John, Member
  Penske, Roger, Member
  Raymond, Lee, Member
  Shipley, Walter, Graduate Member
  Weill, Sanford, Graduate Member

Business Council on National Issues: Culver, David, Former Chairman

Business Enterprise Trust: Buffett, Warren, Trustee

Business Roundtable: Robinson, James, Co-Chair
  Jones, Reginald, Former Co-Chairman
  Bechtel, Riley, Member
  Chenault, Kenneth, Member
  David, George, Member
  Dorman, David, Member
  Ford, Scott, Member
  Galvin, Christopher, Former Member
  Harrison, William, Member
  Houghton, James R., Member
  Immelt, Jeffrey, Member
  Mettler, Ruben, Member
  Raymond, Lee, Member
  Ryan, Arthur, Member
  Purcell, Philip, Member
  Welch, John, Former Member

Buy.com: Ingram, David, Former Director

C2, Incorporated: Brady, Nicholas, Director

Cabot Microelectronics Corporation: Fuller, H. Laurance, Director

CAI Capital Corporation: Culver, David, Chairman

California Institute of Technology: Bechtel, Steve, Trustee
    Biaggini, Benjamin, Trustee
    Beall, Donald, Trustee

Callaway Golf Company: Armacost, Samuel, Director

Calpine Corporation: Derr, Kenneth, Director

Caltech: Cooley, Richard, Trustee Emeritus

Capital Cities/ABC: Murphy, Thomas, CEO, Retired

Capital National Bank: Farish, William, Founding Director

Cardinal Health, Incorporated: Knight, Lester, Director and Former Vice Chairman

Carlisle Companies, Incorporated: Ford, Scott, General Counsel and Vice President

Carnegie Hall: Weill, Sanford, Chairman
    David, George, Trustee

Carolina Citizens Freedom Foundation: Belk, John, Advisory Council

Carolinas' Partnership: Belk, John, Member

Castle Pines Golf Club: Vickers, Jack, Founder

Castle Rock Foundation: Coors, Peter, Trustee

Catalyst: Bryan, John, Director
    Harrison, William B., Director
    Immelt, Jeffrey, Director
    Galvin, Christopher, Former Director

Caterpillar: Fites, Donald, Chairman and CEO, Retired
    Morgan, Lee, Chairman and CEO, Retired
    Goode, David, Director

CBS: Jordan, Michael, Chairman and CEO, Retired

Center for Advanced Studies in Behavioral Sciences: Reed, John, Trustee

Center for Strategic and International Studies: Nunn, Sam, Chairman

Centerre Trust: Williams, Eugene, Chairman, Retired

Central Atlanta Progress: Driver, Walter, Member

Central Southwest: Howell, William, Director

Cessna Aircraft Company of Wichita: Lewis, David, Former Director

CF Foundation: Cousins, Thomas, Trustee and Former Chair

Chamber of Commerce of the United States: Chapman, Hugh, Former Director

Character Education Partnership: de Windt, E. Mandell, Donor

Charles Bulfinch Society: Beach, Morrison, Chair

Charles Schwab Corporation: Shultz, George, Director

Charlotte Airport Advisory Committee: Belk, John, Former Chairman

Charlotte Regional Partnership: Harris, John, Chairman

Charlotte World Affairs Council: Belk, John, Former Director

Charlotte-Mechlenburg Hospital Authority: Harris, John, Director

Charter-Triad Terminals, LLC: Boardman, Clayton, Chairman

Chase Manhattan Bank: Shipley, Walter, Chairman of the Board, Retired
    LeBlond, Richard, Retired
    Ryan, Arthur, Former President
    Love, Ben, Advisory Director

Chemical Bank of New York: Rice, W. Thomas, Former Director

Chemical Banking Corporation: McGillicuddy, John, Former CEO and Chairman

ChevronTexaco: Granville, Maurice, Chairman and CEO, Retired
    Kinnear, James, President and CEO, Retired
    McKinley, John, Chairman and CEO, Retired
    Haynes, Harold, CEO, Retired
    Derr, Kenneth, Chairman and CEO, Retired
    Nunn, Sam, Director
    Armacost, Samuel, Director
    Bower, Donald, Retired
    Rambin, J. Howard, Retired

Chicago Symphony Orchestra: Searle, William, Trustee
    Seaman, Irving, Trustee

ChoicePoint, Incorporated: Murray, J. Terrence, Director

Christie Cookie Company: Wilt, Toby, Chairman

Chrysler Corporation: Bryan, Anthony, Former Director

Chubb Corporation: Stone, Robert, Former Director

Churchill Downs, Incorporated: Farish, William, Former Chairman

Citigroup: Weill, Sanford, Chairman and Former CEO
    Reed, John, Former CEO
    Derr, Kenneth, Director
    David, George, Director
    Remey, Donald, Former Executive, various positions, Citibank
    Houghton, Amory, Former Director, Citicorp
    Garvin, Clifton, Former Director, Citicorp
    Reed, John, Chairman, Citicorp and Citibank, N.A., Retired
    Haynes, Harold, Former Director, Citicorp-Citibank
    Budd, Edward, Chairman and CEO, Travelers, Retired
    Beach, Morrison, Travelers, Retired

Citizens Bancshares: Robinson, Ray, Chairman

City of Charlotte, NC: Belk, John, Former Mayor

Clean Diesel Technologies, Incorporated: Bailey, Ralph, Director

Cleveland State University: de Windt, E. Mandell, Former Trustee

Club Car: Reynolds, John, title unavailable

Coca-Cola Company: Buffett, Warren, Director
   Nunn, Sam, Director
   Robinson, James, Director
   Belk, John, Former Director, Coca-Cola Bottling
   Johnson, Crawford, Retired, Coca-Cola Bottling
   Nielsen, Claude, President and CEO, Coca-Cola Bottling United
   Cousins, Thomas, Venture Business Associate

Coil Coaters of America: Troutman, Frank, title unavailable

Colby College: Pugh, Lawrence, Trustee

Cold Spring Harbor Laboratory: Danforth, Theodore, Former Director

Colgate University: Remey, Donald, Trustee Emeritus

College Football Hall of Fame: Broyles, Frank, Member, Arkansas Hall of Fame

Colonial Properties Trust: Nielsen, Claude, Director

Colorado National Bankshares, Incorporated: Nicholson, Will, Former CEO

Columbia Nitrogen: Copenhaver, William, Chairman, Retired

Columbus Bank and Trust Company: Blanchard, James, Director

Columbus State University Foundation: Blanchard, James, Trustee

Commerce Club of Atlanta: Payne, William, Director

Commission on Marine Science, Engineering and Resources: Baldwin, Robert, Former Member

Committee for Economic Development: Robinson, James, Member
   Adam, Ray, Honorary Trustee
   Blauvelt, Howard, Honorary Trustee

Committee to Encourage Corporate Philanthropy: Derr, Kenneth, Co-Chairman
   Buffett, Warren, Member
   Chenault, Kenneth, Member
   Coors, Peter, Member
   David, George, Member
   Gerstner, Louis, Member
   Goode, David, Member
   Immelt, Jeffrey, Member
   Knight, Charles, Member
   Lewis, Kenneth, Member
   Murphy, Thomas, Member
   Purcell, Philip, Member
   Ryan, Arthur, Member
   Shipley, Walter, Member
   Warner, Douglas, Member
   Weill, Sanford, Member

Communications Satellite Corporation: Laird, Melvin, Former Director

Community Foundation for the Central Savannah River Area: Copenhaver, William, Honorary Director
   Evans, Nick, Director
   Blanchard, Thomas, Director

Comprehensive Software Systems, Incorporated: Stephens, Warren, Director

Compressor Components Textron: Dolan, Beverly, President, Retired

Conexant Systems, Incorporated: Beall, Donald, Director

Connecticut Higher Education Supplemental Loan Authority: Beach, Morrison, Former Director

Conoco: Bailey, Ralph, Former Chairman and CEO
    Blauvelt, Howard, Retired

Conservation Fund Corporate Council: Bechtel, Riley, Member

Consumer Venture Partners: Hillman, Henry, Capital Provider

Copperweld Corporation: Bryan, Anthony, Former Chairman and CEO

Core Industries, Incorporated: Stone, Robert, Former Director

Cornell University: Weill, Sanford, Business Council
    Derr, Kenneth, Trustee Emeritus
    Fuller, H. Laurance, Trustee

Corning, Incorporated: Houghton, James, Chairman of the Board and CEO
    Houghton, Amory, Former CEO
    Perkins, Donald, Former Director
    Stone, Robert, Former Director

Council on Competitiveness: Mettler, Ruben, Member

Council on Foreign Relations: Peterson, Peter, Chairman
    Boeschenstein, William, Member
    Chenault, Kenneth, Member
    Daniel, D. Ronald, Member
    de Windt, E. Mandell, Member
    Derr, Kenneth, Member
    Gerstner, Louis, Director
    Godchaux, Frank, Member
    Goode, David, Director
    Granville, Maurice, Member
    Grune, George, Member
    Houghton, James, Member
    McCartan, Patrick, Member
    McKinley, John, Member
    Murphy, Thomas, Member
    Opel, John, Member
    Raymond, Lee, Member
    Robinson, James, Member
    Shultz, George, Member

Cousins Properties: Cousins, Thomas, Cofounder and Chairman
    Payne, William, Director
    McColl, Hugh, Director
    Knox, Boone, Former Director

Cox Communications: Kirtland, Clifford, Former Chair, President and CEO

Cox Enterprises: Rizzo, Paul, Director
    Love, Ben, Former Director

Credit Suisse First Boston: Poling, Harold, Executive Advisory Board

Crescent Publishing Company, LLC: Wearn, Wilson, Former Director

Crescent Real Estate Equities Company: Anderson, Lyle, Business Associate

Crown Media, Incorporated: Hoak, James, Former CEO

CSRA Community Foundation: Boardman, Clayton, Director

CT Realty: Beall, Donald, Director

CVS Corporation: Murray, J. Terrence, Director

Daimler-Chrysler: Gerstner, Louis, Advisory Board

Dallas Foundation: Chambers, James, Former Governor
  Keay, James, Former Governor
  Stewart, Robert, Former Governor

Dallas Times Herald: Chambers, James, Publisher

Dan River: Lanier, Joseph, Chairman and CEO

Daniel Stowe Botanical Garden: Belk, John, Director

Davidson College: Belk, John, Trustee

Davis Cabinet: Davis, W. Lipscomb, Principal

Dayton Foundation: Oelman, Robert, Former Board Member

Del Monte Foods Company: Armacost, Samuel, Director

Dell Computer Corporation: Nunn, Sam, Director
  Jordan, Michael, Director

Delphi Corporation: Colbert, Virgis, Director
  Penske, Roger, Director

Delta Air Lines, Incorporated: Goode, David, Director
  Budd, Edward, Director

Denver Art Museum: Hamilton, Frederic, Trustee

Detroit Lions, Incorporated: Ford, William, Vice Chairman

Detroit Renaissance Foundation: Ford, William, Vice Chairman

Deutsche Bank Trust Corporation: Howell, William, Director

Devon Energy Corporation: Fluor, Peter, Director

Dial Corporation: Ford, Joe, Director

Dillards, Incorporated: Stephens, Warren, Director

DIMON, Incorporated: Johnson, James, Director
  Lanier, Joseph, Director
  Dickson, R. Stuart, Director

Division I Athletic Directors Association: Broyles, Frank, Former Chairman, Executive Committee Member

DMB Real Estate: Anderson, Lyle, Business Associate

Donaldson, Lufkin & Jenrette: Poling, Harold, Investment Banking Advisory Board

DoubleClick, Incorporated: Murphy, Thomas, Director

Doubleday & Company, Incorporated: Doubleday, Nelson, Former President

Doubletree Corporation & Partners: Ferris, Richard, Former Co-Chairman

Evanston Northwestern Healthcare: Knight, Lester, Director

Exelon Corporation: Brennan, Edward, Director

Exponent, Incorporated: Armacost, Samuel, Director

ExxonMobil: Raymond, Lee, Chairman and CEO
    Garvin, Clifton, Chairman, Retired
    Shipley, Walter, Director
    Houghton, James, Director
    Howell, William, Director
    Fites, Donald, Director
    Warner, Rawleigh, Retired

Eyesight Foundation of Alabama: Thompson, Hall W., Trustee

Federal Express: Bryan, Anthony, Former Director

Federal Reserve: Lilly, David, Former Board of Governors
    Ford, Scott, Chairman, Bank Little Rock Branch
    Peterson, Peter, Chairman, Bank of New York
    Opel, John, Former Chairman, Bank of New York

Federated Department Stores: Peterson, Peter, Former Director

Fieldcrest Mills: Battle, William, Former Chairman and CEO

Fifty Associates: Moseley, Frederick, Director

Financial Services Forum: Harrison, William, Member
    Lewis, Kenneth, Member
    Purcell, Philip, Member
    Ryan, Arthur, Member

Financial Services Roundtable: Lewis, Kenneth, Board Member
    Blanchard, James, Former Director

Financial Services Volunteer Corps: Opel, John, Steering Committee

First Alabama Bancshares: Blount, William, Director

First Alabama Bank of Birmingham: Blount, William, Director

First City National Bank of Houston: Bryan, Anthony, Former Director

First Data Corporation: Robinson, James, Director

First Federal Savings & Loan of Grand Forks: Bridston, Paul, Former President and CEO

First Source Corporation: Wilt, Toby, Director

First Tee of Lakeland: Ridley, Fred, Member of Advisory Board

First Union: Cousins, Thomas, Former Director

Fisk University: Colbert, Virgis, Trustee

Fleet Financial Group: Murray, J. Terrence, CEO, Retired

FleetBoston Financial Corporation: Murray, J. Terrence, Director

FlexSol, Incorporated: Wearn, Wilson, Former Director

Flint Ink Corporation: Poling, Harold, Director

Florida Rock Industries: Rice, W. Thomas, Former Director

Flowers Industries, Incorporated: Lanier, Joseph, Director

Fluor Corporation: Fluor, Peter, Lead Independent Director

FMC Technologies, Incorporated: Bowlin, Mike, Director

Foley & Lardner: Ridley, Fred, Partner

Ford Motor: Ford, William Clay, Director, Former Vice Chair
    Poling, Harold, Chairman and CEO, Retired
    Hampson, Robert, Retired
    Reitzle, Wolfgang, Former Head, Ford Motor (PAG)

FORE!: Boardman, Clayton, Director

Forum for Corporate Conscience: McColl, Hugh, Chairman
    Lewis, Kenneth, Board of Advisors

Fountainhead Water: Wislar, George, Founder

Fourjay: Dobbs, John C., position unavailable

Franklin Street Partners: Rizzo, Paul, Chairman and Partner

Franklin Templeton Investments: Johnson, Charles, Chairman

Freeport Center: O'Block, Robert, General Partner

Fremont Group: Haynes, Harold, Director
    Shultz, George, Director
    Bechtel, Riley, Director

Friends of Acadia: Kirkland, David, Donor

Friends of Florida: Boeschenstein, William, Donor
    Boothby, Willard, Donor
    Danforth, Theodore, Donor
    Mansell, Frank, Donor
    Ordway, John, Donor
    Parker, H. Lawrence, Donor

Fuel Tech: Bailey, Ralph, Chairman and CEO

Gannett Television Group: Townsend, Ronald, President, Retired

Gary Concrete Products: Gary, William, Retired

Gates Rubber Company: Gates, Charles, Retired

GD Searle: Searle, William, Chair and CEO, Retired

General Electric: Immelt, Jeffrey, Chairman and CEO
    Welch, John, Chairman and CEO, Retired
    Jones, Reginald, Chairman and CEO, Retired
    Nunn, Sam, Director
    Penske, Roger, Director
    Warner, Douglas, Director
    Parker, Jack, Retired

General Motors: Bryan, John, Director
    Ward, Lloyd, Former Director
    Kennard, Edward, Vice President, Retired

General Parts, Incorporated: McColl, Hugh, Director

Genesco: Davis, W. Lipscomb, Director

Genome Therapeutics Corporation: Loucks, Vernon, Director

GeoQuest International Holdings, Incorporated: Butler, John, Former Chairman and CEO

Georgia Bank and Trust Company: Copenhaver, William, Director

Georgia Chamber of Commerce: Blanchard, James, Director
    Boardman, Clayton, Former Director
    Kuhlke, Dessey, Member
    Douglass, Edwin, Member and Former Director
    Gabrielsen, James, Former Director

Georgia Cities Foundation: Boardman, Clayton, Director

Georgia Golf Hall of Fame: Gabrielsen, James, Member
    Yates, P. Dan, Member
    Yates, Danny, Member

Georgia-Pacific Corporation: Goode, David, Director
    Fites, Donald, Director

Georgia Research Alliance: Blanchard, James, Director
    Cousins, Thomas, Director

Georgia State Bar: Barrett, Hale, Member
    Sanders, Carl, Member

Georgia State Golf Association: Yates, Danny, Former Director
    Yates, P. Dan, Foundation Director and Former Director
    Gabrielsen, James, Former Director

Georgia, State of: Blanchard, James, Chairman, Department of Industry, Trade and Tourism
    Sanders, Carl, Former Governor and State Senator

Georgia Tech: Nunn, Sam, Sam Nunn School of International Affairs

Geraldine R. Dodge Foundation: Baldwin, Robert, Chairman Emeritus

Gertrude Herbert Institute of Art Foundation: Boardman, Clayton, Director

Gibraltar Financial Corporation & Gibraltar Banks: Kirkland, David, Chairman of the Board and Shareholder

Gilead Sciences, Incorporated: Shultz, George, Director

Gleacher Partners, LLC: Payne, William, Partner

Global SantaFe: Shannon, Edfred, Retired

Global Support for Witness Systems, Incorporated: Ford, Joe, Senior Vice President

Gloucester Bank & Trust: Moseley, Frederick, Former Director

Golden Bear International, Incorporated: Anderson, Lyle, Business Associate

Goldman Sachs: Weinberg, John, Retired
    Bryan, John, Director

Goodwill Industries, Greater New York & Northern New Jersey: Shipley, Walter, Chairman and Director

Graniteville Company: Timmerman, Robert, position unavailable

Greater Milwaukee Open Golf Tournament: Colbert, Virgis, Director

Green Bay Packers, Incorporated: Colbert, Virgis, Director

Greenfield Village: Ford, William, Chairman of the Board of Trustees

Grinnell College: Buffett, Warren, Trustee

H. J. Heinz Company: Coors, Peter, Director
Usher, Thomas, Director

Halliburton Company: Howell, William, Director
Derr, Kenneth, Director

Hamilton Oil Corporation: Hamilton, Frederic, CEO and Chairman
Bryan, Anthony, Former Director

Harison-Kerzic Insurance: Harison, Phil, Principal

Harper Pennington & Shaw: Harper, Harry, Principal

Hartwick College: Anderson, Warren, Counsel

Harvard University: Daniel, D. Ronald, Chairman, Harvard Management Company
Moseley, Frederick, Former VP and Director, Alumni Association
Houghton, Amory, Former Member, Board of Overseers
Houghton, James, Member, Harvard Corporation
Daniel, D. Ronald, Member, Former Treasurer, Harvard Corporation
Stone, Robert, Senior Fellow, Harvard Corporation
Chenault, Kenneth, Law School Dean's Advisory Board

Hauser Richards & Company: Richards, Ruben, Former Principal

Hawaii State Junior Golf Association: Erdman, C. Pardee, Sponsor

HBW Holdings, Incorporated: Hoak, James, Former Chairman

HCA Corporation: MacNaughton, Donald, President, Retired
Gluck, Frederick, Director

Health Management Associates, Incorporated: Lewis, Kenneth, Director

HealthCare Chaplaincy: Herlihy, Edward, Trustee

Henry Ford Museum: Ford, William, Chairman of the Board of Trustees

Hercules, Incorporated: Kennedy, Robert, Director

Heritage Communications: Hoak, James, Former Chairman

High Museum of Art in Atlanta: Cousins, Thomas, Former President and Trustee

Hilb, Rogal and Hobbs Company: O'Brien, Thomas, Director

Hillman Company: Hillman, Henry, Venture Capitalist

Hillsboro Enterprises: Davis, W. Lipscomb, Partner

Hinman, Howard & Kattell, LLP: Anderson, Warren, Partner

Historic Augusta: Boardman, Clayton, Director

Hoak Capital Corporation: Hoak, James, Chairman

Hoblitzelle Foundation: Keay, James, Honorary Life Member

Home Depot, Incorporated: Penske, Roger, Director

Homeownership Education and Counseling Institute: Lewis, Kenneth, Director

Honeywell: Bossidy, Lawrence, Retired

Hoover Institution: Derr, Kenneth, Board of Overseers
Beall, Donald, Board of Overseers

Horatio Alger Assocation: Beall, Donald, Member
  Cousins, Thomas, Member
  Stephens, Jackson, Member
  Roderick, David, Member

Hormel Foods Corporation: Waller, Robert, Director

Hospital Corporation International: Bryan, Anthony, Former Director

Houston Advanced Research Center: Butler, John, Director

Houston Parks Board: Farish, William, Chairman

Howard Heinz Endowment: Love, Howard, Trustee

Howerdd Group: Howerdd, Eugene, Principal

Hull, Towill, Norman, Barrett & Salley: Barrett, Hale, Partner

i2 Technologies, Incorporated: Jordan, Michael, Director

IBM: Gerstner, Louis, Former Chairman and CEO
  Rizzo, Paul, Former Director and CFO
  Akers, John, Former Chairman and CEO
  Opel, John, Former Chairman and CEO
  Chenault, Kenneth, Director
  Knight, Charles, Director
  Houghton, Amory, Former Director
  Cousins, Thomas, Venture Business Associate

ICOS Corporation: Gates, William, Director

ILD Telecommunications, Incorporated: Payne, William, Director

Illinois Coalition for Science and Technology: Galvin, Christopher, Director

Imetal: Bryan, Anthony, Former Director

iMotors: Ward, Lloyd, Former Chairman and CEO

Imperial Chemical Industries plc: Hampel, Ronald, Former Chairman and CEO

Inc. Limited: Thompson, Richard, Director

Indian School of Business: Bechtel, Riley, Governing Board Member

Infinity Pharmaceuticals: Daniel, D. Ronald, Director

InfraReDx, Incorporated: Marquard, William, Director

Ingram Entertainment: Ingram, David, Chairman and President

Ingram Micro: Ingram, David, Former Director

Inman Mills: Chapman, Robert, President
  Chapman, Hugh, Director

Institute for International Economics: Peterson, Peter, Founding Chairman

Intelligent Life Corporation: O'Block, Robert, Director

InterCept Group, Incorporated: Knox, Boone, Former Director

International Federation of Newspaper Publishers: Anderson, Harold, Former Head

International Golf Federation: Ridley, Fred, Joint Chair

International Paper Company: Kennedy, Robert, Director

International Speedway: Penske, Roger, Vice Chairman of the Board

International Star Class Yacht Racing Association: Cross, Rex, Life Member

Internet Security Systems, Incorporated: Nunn, Sam, Director

Ireland Funds: Herlihy, Edward, Member of Chairman's Committee

ITT Corporation: Bryan, Anthony, Former Director

Ivy Foundation for Biomedical Research, University of Virginia: Battle, William, Retired

J.C. Penney: Howell, William, Chairman Emeritus

JPMorgan Chase & Company: Harrison, William, Chairman and CEO
  Warner, Douglas, Former Board Chair
  Fuller, H. Laurance, Director
  Bechtel, Riley, Director
  Raymond, Lee, Director
  Bossidy, Lawrence, Director
  Shultz, George, Chairman, International Advisory Council
  Fluor, Peter, Advisory Board
  Adam, Ray, Partner, Retired, JPMorgan and Company
  Culver, David, Former Director, International Council, JPMorgan and Company
  Bailey, Ralph, Former Director, JPMorgan and Company
  Stewart, Robert, Vice Chairman, Bank One, Retired
  Warren, William, Former Director, Bank One
  Bryan, John, Director, Bank One

J. R. Butler and Company: Butler, John, Chairman and CEO

Japan Airlines: Anderson, Lyle, Business Associate

JASON Foundation for Education: Bechtel, Riley, Trustee

Jazz Semiconductor: Beall, Donald, Director

Jefferson Pilot Corporation: Payne, William, Director

Jewel Cos.: Perkins, Donald, CEO, Retired

JLCM: Richards, Ruben, Senior Managing Director

Jockey Club: Mansell, Frank, Member
  Reynolds, David, Member

Johnson & Johnson: Rizzo, Paul, Former Director

Johnson C. Smith University: Hance, James, Visitor's Board

Jones, Day, Reavis & Pogue: McCartan, Patrick, Former Managing Partner

Josiah Macy Jr. Foundation: Gilbert, S. Parker, Director

JP Stevens and Company: Stevens, Whitney, Former Chairman

JTL Corporation: Lupton, John, Chairman

Judicial Conference of the United States: McCartan, Patrick, Member

Junior Achievement of Chicago: Knight, Lester, Director

Jupiter Medical Center Foundation: Mansell, Frank, Trustee

Justin Brands: Buffett, Warren, Chairman

Juvenile Diabetes Foundation: Belk, John, Advisory Board Member

K2 Incorporated: Holtz, Lou, Director

Kelman Technology, Incorporated: Butler, John, Director

Kelso & Company, Incorporated: McGillicuddy, John, Director
  Marquard, William, Former Director

King & Spalding Law Firm: Driver, Walter, President
  Nunn, Sam, Senior Partner

Kirby Corporation: Stone, Robert, Chairman Emeritus

Kiwanis of Augusta: Battey, Louis, Member
  Barrett, Hale, Member
  Blanchard, Thomas, Member
  Roberts, Julian, Member

Kmart Corporation: Kennedy, Robert, Director

Knight Ridder: Weinberg, John, Director

Knightsbridge Fine Wines, Incorporated: Bryan, Anthony, Director

Knox College: Fites, Donald, Trustee

Knox Foundation: Knox, Jefferson, Principal

Koppers Corporation: Bryan, Anthony, Former Director
  Oelman, Robert, Retired

KSL Recreation Corporation: Hazen, Paul, Director

Kuhlke Investment Company, LLC: Kuhlke, Dessey, CEO

Lake Forest Open Lands Assocation: Wood, Arthur, Donor

Lakeside Cable TV, Incorporated: Wearn, Wilson, Former CEO

LaSalle Hotel Properties: Perkins, Donald, Director

Laureate Building Corporation: Warren, William, CEO

Lehman Brothers Holdings, Incorporated: Akers, John, Director
  Culver, David, Former Director

Liberty Mutual: Chapman, Robert, Former Director

Lincoln Harris: Harris, John, President

Linde AG: Reitzle, Wolfgang, position unavailable

Lone Star Industries: Cross, Rex, Retired

Louisiana Land and Exploration: Phillips, John, Retired

Lowe's Companies, Incorporated: Lewis, Kenneth, Director

LTV Steel Company: Jones, E. Bradley, Chairman and CEO, Retired

Lucent Technologies: Perkins, Donald, Former Director
  McGinn, Richard, Former Chairman and CEO

Lyle Anderson Company: Anderson, Lyle, Founder and Chairman

Maersk: Rizzo, Paul, Director

Main Street Augusta: Boardman, Clayton, Director

Manitowoc Company, Incorporated: Colbert, Virgis, Director

Manor Care, Incorporated: Colbert, Virgis, Director

Manufacturers Hanover: McGillicuddy, John, CEO, Retired

Marathon Oil Corporation: Usher, Thomas, Chairman

March of Dimes: Hance, James, Director

Marshall & Ilsey: Baur, Andrew, Director

Martin Marietta: Laird, Melvin, Former Director

Massachusetts Institute of Technology, Corporation of the: Reed, John, Member

Masters Golf Tournament: Norvell, J. Fleming, Committee Member

Matria Healthcare, Incorporated: Sanders, Carl, Director

May Department Stores Company: Whitacre, Edward, Director

Mayo Clinic: Waller, Robert, President Emeritus
    Warner, Rawleigh, Trustee Emeritus

Maytag Corporation: Ward, Lloyd, Former Chairman and CEO

McColl Brothers Lockwood: McColl, Hugh, Chairman

McDonald's Corporation: Brennan, Edward, Director

McDonnell Douglas/General Dynamics: Lewis, David, Former Chairman and CEO

McGill University Health Centre in Montreal: Culver, David, Chairman

McKinsey & Company: Daniel, D. Ronald, Partner
    O'Block, Robert, Partner, Retired
    Gluck, Frederick, Consultant

Mead Corporation of Dayton, Ohio: Lewis, David, Former Director

Mediacom Communications: Morris, William, Director

Memorial Sloan-Kettering Cancer Center: Warner, Douglas, Chairman
    Robinson, James, Honorary Co-Chair
    Kinnear, James, Director
    Harrison, William, Director
    Weinberg, John, Director
    Weill, Sanford, Director
    Garvin, Clifton, Former Board of Overseers Member

Memphis University School: Dobbs, John H., Trustee

Merck & Company, Incorporated: Bossidy, Lawrence, Director
    Harrison, William, Director

Mesa Limited Partnership: Pickens, Boone, Founder and Chairman

Metropolitan Life Insurance Company: Houghton, James, Director
    Adam, Ray, Former Director
    Laird, Melvin, Director's Advisory Council

Metropolitan Museum of Art: Houghton, James, Trustee

Microsoft Corporation: Gates, William, Chairman and Chief Software Architect

Miller Brewing Company: Colbert, Virgis, Executive Vice President

Mindspeed Technologies: Beall, Donald, Director

Minnesota Mining and Manufacturing Company: Brennan, Edward, Director

Minnesota Museum of American Art: Lilly, Bruce, Director

Minnesota Public Radio: Lilly, Bruce, Trustee

Minnesota Vikings: Whitney, Wheelock, Former Owner, Retired

Mirant Corporation: Robinson, Ray, Director

Mississippi Valley Bancshares: Baur, Andrew, Chairman, Southwest Bank of St. Louis

Mobil Corporation: Anderson, Lyle, Business Associate

Mocksville Cable TV, Incorporated: Wearn, Wilson, Former CEO

Moravian College: Foy, Lewis, Life Trustee

Morgan Guarantee Trust Company: Bailey, Ralph, Director, Retired

Morgan Guaranty Trust: Adam, Ray, Director, Retired

Morgan Stanley: Purcell, Philip, Chairman and CEO
 Knight, Charles, Director
 Brennan, Edward, Director
 Rizzo, Paul, Former Director
 Baldwin, Robert, Chairman, Retired
 Gilbert, S. Parker, Chairman, Retired
 Parker, H. Lawrence, Retired, Morgan Stanley Canada

Morris Communications: Morris, William, Chairman and CEO

Morris Multimedia: Morris, Charles, President and CEO

Moses Contracting: Yates, Charles, position unavailable

Motorola, Incorporated: Galvin, Christopher, Former Chairman and CEO
 Fuller, H. Laurance, Director
 Warner, Douglas, Director

Mount Sinai–New York University: Chenault, Kenneth, Director

MRYP: Knox, Boone, Director

MS Foundation of Georgia: Hudson, W. Howard, Board Member

Multimedia Incorporated: Wearn, Wilson, Retired

N.Y. Telephone: Houghton, Amory, Former Director

Nanophase Technologies Corporation: Perkins, Donald, Chairman

Nashville Bank and Trust Company: Davis, W. Lipscomb, Organizer

National Academy Foundation: Weill, Sanford, Chairman
 Robinson, James, Director
 David, George, Director
 Chenault, Kenneth, Director

National Academy of Engineering: Welch, John, Former Chairman
 Lewis, David, Fellow
 Mettler, Ruben, Member

National Action Council for Minorities in Engineering: Bechtel, Steve, Founder
 Morrow, Richard, Chairman Emeritus
 Heckert, Richard, Board Member Emeritus
 Opel, John, Board Member Emeritus

National Association of Broadcasters Television: Townsend, Ronald, Former Chairman

Nuclear Threat Initiative: Nunn, Sam, CEO and Co-Chairman
    Buffett, Warren, Advisor to the Board of Directors

NYNEX Corporation: Shipley, Walter, Director, Retired

Ocean Energy, Incorporated: Fluor, Peter, Former Director

Ohio Business Roundtable: McCartan, Patrick, Member

Omaha World-Herald Company: Anderson, Harold, Former Chairman of the Board

Omega Polymer Technologies: Wearn, Wilson, Former Director

Ontario Power Generation, Incorporated: Thompson, Richard, Director

Orthopaedic Associates: Hudson, W. Howard, Physician

Oshkosh Truck Corporation: Fites, Donald, Director

Outback Steakhouse: Ridley, Fred, Director, Champions Tour Tournament
    Wilt, Toby, Director

Owens-Corning: Boeschenstein, William, President and CEO, Retired

Oxford Bioscience: Danforth, Theodore, Retired

Oxford Industries: Reith, Carl, Retired

PACCAR: Pigott, Mark, Chairman and CEO
    Pigott, Charles, Chairman Emeritus
    Haynes, Harold, Former Director
    Cooley, Richard, Former Director

Paine Webber: Mansell, Frank, Retired
    Boothby, Willard, Retired

Pan American World Airways, Incorporated: Love, Ben, Former Director

PanAmSat Corporation: Hoak, James, Director

Peachtree Golf Club, Atlanta: Gabrielsen, James, Former President

Pebble Beach Company: Ferris, Richard, Co-Chair

Penn Engineering and Manufacturing Corporation: Boothby, Willard, Director

Penske Group: Penske, Roger, Chairman and CEO

PepsiCo, Incorporated: Ward, Lloyd, Former Executive, various positions
    Akers, John, Director
    Allen, Robert, Director
    Stewart, Robert, Former Director

Perkin-Elmer Corporation: Kennedy, Robert, Retired

Petroleum Information Corporation: Butler, John, Former Senior Chairman

Pfingsten Partners, LLC: Boeschenstein, William, Executive Limited Partner

Pfizer, Incorporated: Howell, William, Director

PGA Tour, Incorporated: Ferris, Richard, Chairman, Policy Board

Pharmaceutical Manufacturers Association: Searle, Daniel, Director

Philadelphia Orchestra Association: Boothby, Willard, Director Emeritus

Phillips Petroleum Company: Laird, Melvin, Former Director

Pier 1 Imports, Incorporated: Hoak, James, Director

Ripplewood Holdings, LLC: Daniel, D. Ronald, Chairman

Riviana Foods: Godchaux, Frank, Chairman of the Board

Robert Boyle Society: Heckert, Richard, Member

Robin Hood: Immelt, Jeffrey, Director

Rockefeller University: Daniel, D. Ronald, Honorary Trustee

Rockwell Collins, Incorporated: Beall, Donald, Director
Ferris, Richard, Director

Rockwell International: Beall, Donald, CEO and Chairman, Retired

Rocky Mountain BankCard System: Nicholson, Will, Chairman

RoundTable Healthcare Partners: Knight, Lester, Founding Partner

Royal and Ancient Golf Club: Bonallack, Michael,

RPM International, Incorporated: Jones, E. Bradley, Director

RRE Ventures: McGinn, Richard, Partner
Robinson, James, Cofounder, RRE Ventures GP II, LLC

Ruddick: Dickson, Thomas, President and CEO
Dickson, R. Stuart, Chairman of Executive Committee

Rush University Medical Center: Morrow, Richard, Trustee

Russell Reynolds Associates, Incorporated: Gluck, Frederick, Director
Stone, Robert, Former Director

S.C. Manufacturers Alliance: Chapman, Robert, Former President

SA Telecommunications: Richards, Ruben, Director

Safeway, Incorporated: Hazen, Paul, Director

Salomon Brothers: Kirtland, Clifford, Director
Kirkland, David, Former Director of Corporate Finance

Salvation Army: Fites, Donald, Chairman, National Advisory Board

Samford University: Blount, William, School of Business Advisory Board

Santa Fe Southern Pacific: Biaggini, Benjamin, Retired

Sara Lee: Bryan, John, Chairman and CEO, Retired

Sarah Mellon Scaife Foundation: Bryan, Anthony, Director

Saudi Aramco: Haynes, Harold, Director

SBC Communications: Whitacre, Edward, Chairman and CEO
Knight, Charles, Director

SCANA Corporation: Chapman, Hugh, Director

Scientific-Atlanta, Incorporated: Nunn, Sam, Director
Dorman, David, Director

Scripps Foundation for Medicine and Science: Culver, David, International Board Member

Sea Island Company: Blanchard, James, Director

Seaboard Coast Line Industries: Rice, W. Thomas, Chairman and CEO, Retired

Seagram Company, Ltd.: Culver, David, Former Director

Seagull Energy Corporation: Fluor, Peter, Former Director

Sears: Brennan, Edward, Retired
    Wood, Arthur, Retired

Seattle Symphony: Cooley, Richard, Director

Seaward Management: Moseley, Frederick, Director

Securities Industry Association: Moseley, Frederick, Member

Sedgwick Group Development Limited: Gabrielsen, James, Director

Seeds of Hope Foundation: Coors, Peter, Trustee

Segway LLC: Loucks, Vernon, Former CEO

Shaw Industries: Cousins, Thomas, Former Director

Skyworks Solutions: Beall, Donald, Director

Sloan-Kettering Institute: Gerstner, Louis, Chairman

Smith Barney: Norvell, J. Fleming, Senior Vice President of Investments

Smithsonian Institution: Cooley, Richard, Honorary Member, National Board

Society for Independent Gasoline Marketers of America: Boardman, Clayton, Former Director

Society of Exploration Geophysicists Foundation: Butler, John, Former Chairman

Sodisco-Howden Group, Incorporated: Culver, David, Former Director

Sonoco Products Company: McColl, Hugh, Director

Sony Corporation: Peterson, Peter, Director
    Gerstner, Louis, Advisory Board

Sooner Federal Savings and Loan: Warren, William, Former Director

South Carolina, State of: Chapman, Robert, Former Director, Board for Technical Education

Southeastern Natural Sciences Academy: Roberts, Julian, Donor
    Battey, Louis, Member
    Blanchard, Thomas, Donor
    Boardman, Clayton, Donor
    Copenhaver, William, Donor
    Finney, H. Ray, Donor
    Gary, William, Donor
    Harison, Phil, Donor

Southern Methodist University: Howell, William, Chairman, Board of Trustees

Southern Peru Copper Corporation: McGillicuddy, John, Director

Spartan Communications, Incorporated: Evans, Nick, CEO and Chairman, Retired
    Chapman, Robert, Former Director

Spartanburg County Foundation: Chapman, Robert, Director

Spartanburg Regional Medical Center Foundation: Chapman, Robert, Former Chairman

Spatial Sites: Roberts, Julian, position unavailable

Spencer Foundation: Reed, John, Trustee

SRI International: Armacost, Samuel, Chairman

St. Joseph Center for Life: Menk, Peter, Former Treasurer

St. Louis Cardinals: Baur, Andrew, Secretary and Treasurer

St. Paul's Episcopal Church: Barrett, Hale, Chancellor

Standard Oil of California: Bower, Donald, Former President and CEO

Stanford University: Pigott, Charles, Chairman Emeritus
    Bechtel, Riley, Law School Dean's Advisory Council
    Culver, David, Institute for International Studies Advisory Council, Former Member

Stanley Works: Colbert, Virgis, Director

Statesman Life Insurance Company: Blount, William, Director

Stephen W. Brown School of Radiography: Brown, Stephen, Principal

Stephens Group: Stephens, Jackson, Chairman
    Stephens, Warren, President and CEO

Stillman Maynard & Company: Ordway, John, position unavailable

Summit Properties, Incorporated: Hance, James, Director

Sunoco, Incorporated: Kennedy, Robert, Director

SunTrust Bank: Davis, W. Lipscomb, Former Director

Superior TeleCom: Jansing, John, Director

Synovus Financial Corporation: Blanchard, James, CEO and Director

TA Associates: Hillman, Henry, Capital Provider

Tampa Urban Junior Golf Association: Ridley, Fred, Member of Advisory Board

Taubman Centers, Incorporated: Gilbert, S. Parker, Director

Temple-Inland: Cousins, Thomas, Venture Business Associate

Tennessee Golf Foundation: Ingram, David, Chairman, Investment Committee

Texas Commerce Bancshares: Love, Ben, Former Director

Texas Crude Energy, Incorporated: Fluor, Peter, Chairman and CEO

Texas Industries, Incorporated: Belk, John, Former Director
    Hoak, James, Director

Texas Instruments, Incorporated: Goode, David, Director

Texas Medical Center: Love, Ben, Director

Textron Incorporated: Johnson, Charles, President, Cessna Aircraft Company
(subsidiary)
    Dickson, R. Stuart, Director
    Ford, Joe, Director

Thayer Capital Partners: Fites, Donald, Board of Advisors

The Carlyle Group: Gerstner, Louis, Chairman

The Citadel: Rice, W. Thomas, Advisory Board

The Conference Board: Mettler, Ruben, Member

The Field Museum: Searle, William, Trustee

The Reader's Digest Association: Laird, Melvin, Senior Counselor, National and International Affairs

The Williams Companies, Incorporated: Williams, John, Former Chairman of the Board and CEO
Winters, J. Otis, Former Director and Executive Vice President
Anderson, Harold, Director
Williams, Joseph, Director, Retired Chairman of the Board
Bailey, Ralph, Director
Chapman, Hugh, Director
Warren, William, Former Director
Howell, William, Director

Thermadyne Holdings Corporation: Poling, Harold, Director

Thinking Tools, Incorporated: Gluck, Frederick, Director

Third National Bank: Davis, W. Lipscomb, Former Director

Thomas Nelson, Incorporated: Davis, W. Lipscomb, Former Director

Thompson Tractor: Thompson, Hall W., Founder

Thomson Corporation: Thompson, Richard, Director

Thurgood Marshall Scholarship Fund: Colbert, Virgis, Chairman

Time-Warner, Incorporated: Perkins, Donald, Former Director

Times Mirror: Beall, Donald, Former Director

TLC Vision Corporation: Wilt, Toby, Director

Torchmark Corporation: Lanier, Joseph, Director

Toronto-Dominion Bank: Thompson, Richard, Director, Retired Chairman and CEO

Total System Services, Incorporated: Driver, Walter, Director
Blanchard, James, Director
Cousins, Thomas, Director Emeritus

Transcontinental Corporation: Anderson, Lyle, Business Associate

Transtar, Incorporated: Peterson, Peter, Director

Treadco, Incorporated: Marquard, William, Former Director

Tredegar Industries: Rice, W. Thomas, Former Director

Trizec Properties, Incorporated: Thompson, Richard, Member of Audit Committee

Troutman Sanders, LLP: Sanders, Carl, Partner

TRW: Mettler, Ruben, Chairman and CEO, Retired

TSW Investment: Wilt, Toby, President

Tubman Home: Simkins, Leroy, position unavailable

Tufts University: Budd, Edward, Trustee

U.K. Government Committee on Corporate Governance: Hampel, Ronald, Former Chairman

U.S. Bancorp: Coors, Peter, Director

U.S.-Japan Business Council: McCartan, Patrick, Member

U.S. Naval Academy: Kinnear, James, Director, Alumni Association and Foundation

U.S. Ski Team: O'Block, Robert, Director

U.S. Venture Partners: Hillman, Henry, Capital Provider

UCAR International: Kennedy, Robert, Former Chairman

Union Carbide Corporation: Kennedy, Robert, CEO and Chairman, Retired

Union Planters Corporation: Waller, Robert, Director

Union Theological Seminary: Belk, John, Trustee

United Airlines, Incorporated: Ferris, Richard, CEO, Retired
  Cooley, Richard, Former Director

United Auto Group, Incorporated: Penske, Roger, Chairman

United Business Media: Hampel, Ronald, Chairman, Retired

United Energy Corporation: Love, Ben, Former Director

United Negro College Fund: Raymond, Lee, Director
  Hance, James, Director

United Security Bancshares, Incorporated: Harrison, William, Director

United States Chamber of Commerce: Nicholson, Will, Director

United States Golf Association: Ridley, Fred, President
  Driver, Walter, Vice President
  Daniel, D. Ronald, Former Vice President
  Gabrielsen, James, Former Executive Committee Member
  Reinhart, James, Secretary
  Taylor, F. Morgan, Executive Committee Member
  Yates, Danny, Former Junior Golf Committee Director

U.S. Government: Baldwin, Robert, Former Under Secretary of the Navy
  Battle, William, Former Ambassador to Australia
  Brady, Nicholas, Former U.S. Secretary of the Treasury
  Farish, William, U.S. Ambassador to the U.K.
  Houghton, Amory, U.S. Representative (New York)
  Jones, Reginald, Former Chairman, President's Export Council
  Laird, Melvin, Former U. S. Secretary of Defense, Former U.S. Congressman
    (Wisconsin)
  Love, Howard, President's Committee on Industrial Competitiveness, Former Member
  Mettler, Ruben, Former Chairman, President's Science Policy Task Force
  Nunn, Sam, Retired U.S. Senator (Georgia)
  Raymond, Lee, Secretary of Energy Advisory Board Member
  Shultz, George, Former U.S. Secretary of State

United States Olympic Committee: Ward, Lloyd, Former CEO

United States Steel Corporation: Usher, Thomas, Chairman and CEO
  McGillicuddy, John, Director

United Technologies/Otis Elevators: David, George, Chairman and CEO

United Way of Atlanta: Driver, Walter, Former Chair, Legal Division

United Way of Dallas: Chambers, James, Life Honorary Board Member

United Way Services of Greater Cleveland: de Windt, E. Mandell, Life Director

Universal Technical Institute, Incorporated: Penske, Roger, Director

University of Arkansas: Broyles, Frank, Director of Athletics

William K. Warren Foundation: Warren, William, Chairman

Willis: Wallace, J. Bransford, Chairman Emeritus

Willis Group, Ltd.: Hazen, Paul, Director

Winn-Dixie Stores: Townsend, Ronald, Director

Wisconsin Alumni Research Foundation: Raymond, Lee, Trustee

Wolverine World Wide, Incorporated: Fites, Donald, Director

Womble Carlyle Sandridge & Rice: Johnson, James, Partner, Retired

Woodrow Wilson International Center for Scholars: Warner, Rawleigh, Trustee

Woodruff Arts Center: Reith, Carl, Life Trustee

World Access, Incorporated: Sanders, Carl, Director

World Amateur Golf Council: Bonallack, Michael, Former Secretary General

World Methodist Council: Fites, Donald, Chairman, Financial Development Committee

World Press Freedom Committee: Anderson, Harold, Chairman Emeritus

World Travel and Tourism Council: Robinson, James, Chairman, Retired

Wright Flyer Over the Carolinas: Belk, John, Chairman

Wright State University: Oelman, Robert, Former President

Wyeth: Shipley, Walter, Director

Xstrata AG: Hazen, Paul, Director

Yates Insurance Agency: Yates, Danny, Principal
Yates, P. Dan, Retired

Young Women's Christian Association: Blount, William, Trustee

Yum! Brands Incorporated: Daniel, D. Ronald, Former Director
Weinberg, John, Director

Zalev Metals, Incorporated: Culver, David, Former Director

NOTES

1. Kraham, Bonnie. "Discrimination Against Women at Private Golf Clubs" (independent research paper, University of Miami School of Law, 1994), p. 8. Citing Katherine E. Speyer, *New York State Club Association v. City of New York: The Demise of the All-Male Club,* 10 Pace L. Rev. 273, 273 (1990), citing among others the Amicus Curiae brief of the American Bar Association supporting *City of New York in New York State Club Association v. City of New York,* 108 S. Ct 2225 (1988).
2. Schafran, Lynn Hecht. "Welcome to the Club." New York: Women and Foundations Corporate Philanthropy, 1981, p. 9. Citing "Private Clubs and Private Choices," *New York Times* editorial, June 3, 1980.
3. Ibid., pp. 10–11. Citing Hearings before the City Commission on Human Rights, November 13, 1973, pp. 72–78.
4. Ibid., p. 13.
5. Ibid., pp. 3–4.
6. Lev. 27:1–7.
7. Harr, Eric. "Women Go Long," *New York Daily News.* January 13, 2003.
8. Kraham, pp. 15–17.
9. Kraham, p. 21.
10. Kraham, p. 22. Citing Richard J. Byrne, *Infringement on the Constitutional Rights to Freedom of Association of the Members of the All Male Rotary International Is Justified Since the State Has a Compelling Interest in Eradicating Discrimination Against Women and in Assuring Them Equal Access to Public Accommodations—*

Board of Directors of Rotary International v. Rotary Club, 107.
S. Ct. 1940 (1987). 38 Drake Law Rev. 157 (1988–89).

11. Kraham, p. 23. Citing Robert Johnson, *Board of Directors of Rotary International v. Rotary Club of Duarte: Redefining Associational Rights,* 1988 B.Y.U.L. Rev. 141, 141 n.2. (1988).

12. Clanton, Angela. "Freedom of Association v. Anti-Discrimination: Is it Legal for the Augusta National Golf Club to Exclude Women From Membership Because of Their Gender?" (independent research paper, 2002), p. 11. Citing *Boy Scouts of America v. Dale,* 530 U.S. 649–50 (2000).

13. Ibid., p. 12. Citing "Freedom of Association: Members Only; Debating Which Private Clubs Are Acceptable and Private," *The New York Times.* December 2002.

14. Owen, David. *The Making of the Masters.* New York: Simon & Schuster, 1999.

15. Women contacting NCWO cited a 1999 agreement between Ford and the Equal Employment Opportunity Commission in which the company agreed to pay $7.75 million to resolve allegations of sexual harassment pursued by the EEOC on behalf of female employees at two Chicago-area plants. They charged that despite anti–sexual harassment training required by the agreement, harassment continues and women continue to come forward, as evidenced by several cases that are still pending.

16. Rynecki, David. "Golf and Power," *Fortune.* April 14, 2003.

17. Gilligan, Carol. *In a Different Voice: Psychological Theory and Women's Development.* Cambridge: Harvard University Press, 1993.

18. National Center for Women and Policing. "Police Use of Excessive Force: Taking Gender into Account." Los Angeles: Feminist Majority Foundation, 1999.

19. Citigroup. "Notice of Annual Meeting to Stockholders." New York, March 16, 2004.

20. Samuelson, Robert J. "CEO Welfare," *The Washington Post.* April 30, 2003.

21. In July 2004, John Rigas and his son Timothy Rigas were found guilty by a federal jury of conspiring to loot the cable television company of millions of dollars. The jury deadlocked on securities

and bank fraud charges against Michael Rigas. U.S. Attorney David N. Kelley said his office intends to retry Michael Rigas's case.

22. "Work Experience in 2002—People 15 Years Old and Over by Total Money Earnings in 2002, Age, Race, Hispanic Origin, and Sex." U.S. Census Bureau, Current Population Survey. 2003 Annual Social and Economic Supplement.

23. In April 2004, Kozlowski's first trial ended in a mistrial after a juror received a suspicious note and telephone call during deliberations. In August 2004, a New York judge rejected requests that conspiracy and corruption charges be dropped. A new trial on accusations of stealing $600 million from Tyco was scheduled for January 18, 2005.

24. Anderson, Dave. "Those New Masters Caddies," *The New York Times*. April 10, 1983.

25. Muelier, Rob. "Lord of the Ring," *Augusta Chronicle*. February 10, 2002.

26. Interview with Hootie Johnson, Associated Press. November 11, 2002.

27. Sherr, Lynn. *Failure Is Impossible: Susan B. Anthony in Her Own Words*. New York: Times Books, Random House, 1995.

28. Ibid.

29. "Professor Ruth Bader Ginsburg's Advocacy for Women's Rights at the Supreme Court, 1971–1979." Program notes, The Annual Justice Ruth Bader Ginsburg Distinguished Lecture on Women and the Law, New York. January 29, 2004.

30. Height, Dorothy. *Open Wide the Freedom Gates*. New York: Public Affairs Division of Perseus Book Group, 2003.

31. Interview with James Symington, founding member of the Federal City Club. June 15, 2004.

32. Ibid.

33. Interview with Roxanne Roberts. June 15, 2004.

34. Preceding discussion beginning with protective laws from Raymond F. Gregory. *Women and Workplace Discrimination*. New Brunswick, NJ: Rutgers University Press, 2003.

35. Miles, Rosalind. *The Women's History of the World*. New York: Perennial Library, Harper & Row, 1988.

36. Shipnuck, Alan. *The Battle for Augusta National.* New York: Simon & Schuster, 2004.

37. Ibid.

38. Bingham, Clara, and Laura Leedy Gansler. *Class Action.* New York: Random House, 2002.

39. Gordon, Meryl. "Discrimination at the Top," *Working Woman.* September 1992.

40. Antilla, Susan. *Tales from the Boom-Boom Room.* New York: HarperBusiness, 2003. As is routine in sex discrimination cases, Smith Barney denied guilt even as they agreed to the terms of the settlement.

41. McGeehan, Patrick. "Morgan Stanley and U.S. Agency Fail to Settle Sex Bias Lawsuit," *The New York Times.* April 16, 2003, p.C.4. Even as they agreed to pay $54 million in a settlement, Morgan Stanley denied guilt and cited their placement on the *Working Mother* magazine "best" list.

42. Antilla.

43. Davis, who is no longer with the foundation, declined to name the company, not wanting to hurt the foundation's future prospects.

44. Shipnuck.

45. Faludi, Susan. *Backlash: The Undeclared War Against American Women.* New York: Crown Publishers, 1991.

46. U.S. Department of Labor, Bureau of Labor Statistics. *Employment status of population by sex, marital status, and presences of age of own children.* 2002.

47. Faludi.

48. Ibid.

49. Ibid.

50. Will, George F. "Lies, Damned Lies, and . . . ," *Newsweek.* March 29, 1999.

51. "Women's Figures," *The Wall Street Journal.* January 5, 1997.

52. vos Savant, Marilyn. "Ask Marilyn," *Parade.* December 26, 1999.

53. Conlin, Michelle. "The New Gender Gap," *BusinessWeek.* May 26, 2003.

54. Sadker, David. "An Educator's Primer on the Gender War," *Phi Delta Kappan.* November 2002.

55. Wallis, Claudia. "The Case for Staying Home," *Time*. March 22, 2004.

56. "Workers Real Wages (1947–2001)." LRA Online, *www.labor research.org/charts.php?id=8*. New York: Labor Research Association, 2004.

57. U.S. Department of Labor, Bureau of Labor Statistics. *Current Population Survey*. 2002.

58. Earnings gap data from Stephen J. Rose and Heidi I. Hartmann. "Still a Man's Labor Market: The Long-Term Earnings Gap." Washington, D.C.: Institute for Women's Policy Research, 2004.

59. Executive and board data from Joanne Cleaver and Betty Spence. "NAFE's Top 30 Companies for Executive Women," *NAFE Magazine*. Winter 2004.

60. Parental status of executives from "Diversity Factoids," *DiversityInc*. August/September 2003.

61. Work hour data from "The American Family: Indicators of Economic Stress." New American Foundation, January 2004.

62. Labor force participation and educational data from "Professional Women: Vital Statistics." Department of Professional Employees, AFL-CIO Fact Sheet 2004-1.

63. EEOC complaint statistics from "Charge Statistics FY 1992 Through FY 2003." U.S. Equal Employment Opportunity Commission, 2004. *www.eeoc.gov/stats/charges.html*.

64. U.S. Department of Labor, Bureau of Labor Statistics. *Employment and Earnings*. BLS News, 04-148.

65. Burk, Martha, and Josh Feltman. "How to Get Paid More, Really," *Executive Female*. Janurary/February 1995.

66. U.S. Department of Labor, Bureau of Labor Statistics. *Gender pay gap largest in sales, lowest in farm occupations*. January 24, 2000.

67. Cobble, Dorothy Sue. *The Other Women's Movement: Workplace Justice and Social Rights in Modern America*. Princeton and Oxford: Princeton University Press, 2004.

68. Gregory, Raymond F. *Women and Workplace Discrimination*. New Brunswick, NJ: Rutgers University Press, 2003.

69. Abuses in a number of cases are discussed in the following: Gregory, Raymond F. *Unwelcome and Unlawful*. Ithaca and London: Cornell University Press, 2004. Bingham, Clara, and Laura Leedy

Gansler. *Class Action*. New York: Doubleday, 2002. And Antilla, Susan. *Tales from the Boom-Boom Room*. New York: Harper-Business, 2003.

70. Many employers now force employees to sign mandatory arbitration agreements (it's usually in the fine print on new employee documents) giving up individual rights to sue in any case. Mandatory arbitration does not apply to class actions. Courts have been mixed on upholding the legality of mandatory arbitration agreements for individuals. For a discussion, see Antilla, p. 179.

71. Brady, Diane. "Crashing GE's Glass Ceiling," *BusinessWeek*. July 28, 2003.

72. Letter to NCWO from Citigroup, August 22, 2002.

73. Letter to NCWO from IBM, August 15, 2002.

74. Letter to NCWO from Ford Motor Company, October 22, 2002.

75. Letter to NCWO from Bank of America, October 4, 2002.

76. Hickman, Jonathan. "Best Companies for Minorities," *Fortune*. June 23, 2002.

77. Bernstein, Aaron. "Women's Pay: Why the Gap Remains a Chasm," *BusinessWeek*. June 14, 2004.

78. American Express. *Employee Code of Conduct*. *http://ir.americanexpress.com* (click on "About the Company" and search for "Code of Conduct").

79. Conlin, Michelle, and Aaron Bernstein. "Working and Poor," *BusinessWeek*. May 31, 2004.

80. Ibid.

81. United Food and Commercial Workers. "Wal-Mart's War on Health Care." June 2004. *http://www.ufcw.org/issues_and_actions/walmart_workers_campaign_info/facts_and_figures/walmarton benefits.cfm*

82. McGeehan, Patrick. "Morgan Stanley and U.S. Agency Fail to Settle Sex Bias Lawsuit," *The New York Times*. April 16, 2003.

83. Daniels, Cora. "Women vs. Wal-Mart," *Fortune*. July 21, 2003.

84. *www.stakeholderalliance.org/history.html*

85. Gornick, Janet C., and Marcia K. Meyers. *Families That Work*. New York: Russell Sage Foundation, 2003. P. 117, citing U.S. Office of Personnel Management, 2001.

86. Ibid., p. 294.

87. Ibid., pp. 137–138.

88. Cascone, Lori A. "The Blair Baby Project: First Family Breaks Tradition," *www.momsrefuge.com*. June 2004.

89. Beginning on July 1, 2004, nearly all non-governmental employees in California became eligible to receive paid family leave through a state-administered program (State Disability Insurance) financed through payroll deductions. Workers can collect as much as 55 percent of their salary, up to a maximum of $728 per week.

90. "Women in Suits: America's Rash of Lawsuits on Sexual Discrimination Is Spreading to Europe," *The Economist*. February 28, 2002.

91. "As the Economy Grows, Workers Still on the Short End," Labor Research Association. 2004. LRA Online, *www.laborresearch.org/story.php?id=356*.

92. Hinchcliffe, Raymond H. "The Cost of Turnover," *Recruiter*. LIMRA International, April 2003.

93. Gornick and Meyers, pp. 156–161.

94. Ibid., p. 148.

95. Schafran. P. 11. Citing Ron Howell. "Man's Place," *New York Daily News*. June 4, 1980.

96. Houghton's hometown paper (*The Buffalo News*, October 14, 2002) editorialized against his membership. In 2004 he announced he would not seek reelection. Whether the desire to keep his membership in Augusta National was a factor, no one knows.

97. The pay raise bill ultimately failed to pass the House; the amendment was not submitted when it became clear that the bill would fail.

98. Lippman, Thomas W. "State Dept. Seeks Gains for Women; Albright Is Stressing Rights Concern in Foreign Policy Agenda," *The Washington Post*. March 25, 1997.

99. Nueman, Nancy M. (ed.). *True to Ourselves: A Celebration of Women Making a Difference*. San Francisco: Jossey-Bass Publishers, 1998.

100. Leahy, Rachel. "Forty-Seven Women in Congress, 170 to Go" (briefing paper, Center for Advancement of Public Policy, Washington, D.C., 1994).

ACKNOWLEDGMENTS

It's always hard to know where to start when you are indebted to so many people, and the journey passed through so many phases. But I must begin by thanking journalists Marcia Chambers and Christine Brennan, whose gender lens on discrimination started it all, and to the many other members of the media, both male and female, who saw this as an important story and knew that it was never about golf.

I couldn't have gotten through the media firestorm that defined the Augusta National controversy for nearly two years without the help of my staff, Rebecca Menso and Christopher Turman. Rebecca not only became expert at dealing with a constant barrage of media calls, she fielded torrents of communications from the public (even death threats) with calm confidence. Christopher handled not only his own job as director of our Social Security project, he took on much additional work doing research, helping with media appearances, and stepping in wherever needed. Later, Program Director Ellen Boneparth and Associate Alison Stein expertly kept our office running and policy work in full swing while this book was written. Emily Morgan and Natalia Filipiak provided important research assistance.

The leaders of the groups that constitute the membership of the National Council of Women's Organizations were steadfast as well, despite orchestrated efforts to divide us. I am particularly indebted to Jane Smith of Business and Professional Women/USA, Jackie Woods of the American Association of University Women, Dorothy Height of the National Council of Negro Women, and Heidi Hart-

251

mann of the Institute for Women's Policy Research for speaking out on the issue through radio, television, and the written word. Dr. Hartmann not only served as vice chair of the NCWO, she served as friend-in-chief.

Many of our leaders lent extraordinary support during our time in Atlanta and Augusta. It would have been literally impossible to mount the protest without the strength and expertise of the Feminist Majority and Eleanor Smeal. Alice Cohan was an extraordinary strategist who was there at every phase, unflappable even while negotiating with the sheriff while under the glare of network cameras. Kim Gandy and Terry O'Neill of NOW and C. DeLores Tucker of the National Congress of Black Women were with us in Atlanta and Augusta.

Many other individuals helped as well. Sam Pryor was there when we needed him more than once, with resources and much-needed moral support. Brenda Feigen spent many months of her own time on legal research, and Lynn Hecht Shafran gave us critical background on the legal history of private-club discrimination. Connie Cordovilla and Catherine Hill underwrote their own expenses to make the journey from Washington to Augusta and to bring others. Members of the public sent encouraging notes and contributions, small and large.

Other groups were also invaluable to the effort. NAACP board chair Julian Bond spoke out early in the controversy and lent his organization's support. Reverend Jessie Jackson and Janis Mathis of Rainbow/PUSH made media appearances and provided resources for the protest. The Southern Christian Leadership Conference and Martin Luther King III gave us a venue and support staff for the press conference in Atlanta during Masters week.

Special thanks go to the women and men in Congress who spoke up, especially Representative Carolyn Maloney of New York, who made the trip to stand with us at Augusta. Her leadership in introducing bills to end tax subsidies for discriminatory clubs and to affirm the sense of Congress that holding memberships in discriminatory clubs is improper for public servants will have resonance long after the controversy fades.

Many good people of Georgia were key, especially Stephanie Davis, then with the Atlanta Women's Foundation, and Atlanta mayor Shirley Franklin, who convened a forum for us to talk with local and state leaders. Nancy Boothe of the Feminist Women's Health Network provided us both people and protection, arranging for security personnel and supporters. Jack Batson and Lisa Krisher, and Joyceen Boyle gave us safe haven and sustenance during our time in Augusta.

We could not have prevailed in the courts without the American Civil Liberties Union and the expert legal team they assembled. Jack Batson expertly guided us through the political landscape of the city of Augusta and Augusta National Golf Club. Batson, Gerald Weber of the ACLU, and Jeff Bramlett of Bondurant, Mixson, and Elmore were key to the legal strategy. Sarah Schalf, who argued our case before the Eleventh Circuit, deserves particular thanks. Cyrus Mehri and the Washington law firm of Mehri & Skalet continue to pursue allegations of sex discrimination in Augusta National–related companies through the Women on Wall Street partnership with NCWO, and for that we are very grateful.

Few good books become reality without good book people. This one is no exception. Thanks to my agents, Fifi Oscard and Peter Sawyer, and Melissa Silverstein, who introduced us. Much credit goes to my editor, Lisa Drew, and her excellent staff, for their suggestions, support, and expertise.

Finally, I would like to thank the men in my life. My Dad, Ivan Burk, fielded media questions with dignity at age eighty-three. My sons, Mark Talley and Ed Talley, served as informal advisers on sports media and coached me through hundreds of hours of talk radio. Most crucially, my husband Ralph Estes was there for me through highs and lows, and helped me make it through many nights of anxiety. More than anyone else, he served as friend, guardian, confidant, and supporter. My indebtedness is from the heart.

INDEX